73-9

FISHING
for all

FISHING
for all

EDITED BY
TED DOUGLAS

NEW
ORCHARD

First published in Great Britain in 1983 by
Ward Lock Limited, Villiers House,
41-47 Strand, London WC2N 5JE,
a Cassell company.

This edition specially produced in
1992 for Bookmart Limited,
Mill Hill Industrial Estate, Desford Road,
Endersby, Leicester LE9 5AO

ISBN 1-85079-193-7

Printed in Czechoslovakia by Slovart.

Acknowledgments

The publishers would like to thank the following for providing photographs for the book:

John Bailey page 23; Arthur Clarke pages 11, 27; John Carding page 17; Geoff Chesterman page 67; Nick Cranfield pages 63, 69, 74, 75, 77, 80; John Darling pages 84-5, 86-7, 89, 93, 96-7, 98, 102, 105, 106, 108, 109, 111, 112, 113, 115, 116, 117, 119, 121, 122, 123, 124, 125; Pete Evans page 48; Steve Harper page 18; Neil Nevison page 60; Arthur Oglesby page 72; Barrie Roberts pages 8, 14, 32, 33, 34, 36, 38, 40, 42; John Tarlton page 52; Jim Tyree pages 24-5; John Watson pages 13, 48.

Contents

Part 1   Coarse fishing

1   Tackle and baits   7
2   The coarse fish   18
3   Fishing methods   30
4   Pike   47

Part 2   Flyfishing

5   Tackle for trout fishing   51
6   Brown and rainbow trout in stillwaters   58
7   Brown and rainbow trout in rivers   66
8   Seatrout and salmon   71
9   Grayling   79

Part 3   Shore fishing

10   Tackle   82
11   Baits   95
12   Predators, cod and bass   103
13   Bottom-feeders, wrasse and mullet   119

Chapter 1
Tackle and baits

Tackle

If you are to become a successful angler it is crucial that you develop a total understanding of your tackle set-up. It is not necessary to own the most up-to-date carbon fibre rod or the very latest fast-retrieve fixed spool reel in order to be successful. What is important is that your tackle is used with the maximum amount of efficiency.

Rods

Since the advent of glass fibre some years ago, the construction of fishing rods has become much more sophisticated; so much so, that very few poor rods are made these days. There are exceptions of course, the 6 ft (1.85 m) solid glass rods which some shops sell as 'boys' rods' are a bad investment, they hamper the young angler's progress. If you have a young child, or you are a youngster yourself, who would like to take up the sport, then start off with a 10–13 ft (3–4 m) pole or a 10 ft (3.05 m) rod. Once the young angler has grown to an age or size when he can graduate to a 12–13 ft (3.65–3.95 m) rod, which is the ideal size, the pole or the 10 ft (3.05 m) rod will remain a useful part of his equipment.

In order to be a successful float angler, you must own one or more float rods; these can be 12, 13 or 14 ft (3.65, 3.95 or 4.25 m) in length, depending on your height and preference. Having equipped yourself with a float rod, which you are satisfied suits you, you must now come to terms with it; spend some time getting to know what the rod will do, and make sure that it will suit your specific requirements.

Lines

The top match angler is constantly striving to improve his bait presentation, because he is confronted with having to catch the maximum amount of fish in the minimum amount of time from a very small area of water. The pleasure angler has no such restrictions, so the need to fish with tiny hooks and ultra-fine lines does not apply to the same extent. However, it is worth remembering that because a finer line will allow a bait to fall more naturally through the water, more bites will be encountered by the angler who fishes with a 2 lb (0.90 kg) line than, say, an angler fishing with a 5 lb (2.25 kg) line. 2.5 lb (1.10 kg) reel line with a 1.7 lb (0.77 kg) or 2 lb (0.90 kg) hook length will suffice under most circumstances, but if you happen to be fishing a swim which houses a snag or you are fishing for big fish, then common sense suggests you use a heavier line.

Your choice of line is important: cheap line is a false economy, so always buy quality line. The difference in price between a poor line and a high-quality one is possibly only a matter of a few pence, but the quality line will last you up to six months, depending on how much fishing you do, and will account for many good fish. The cheaper one will show signs of wear very quickly and will invariably cost you a good fish. Something many anglers do not realize is that similar lines often behave differently from one another. Some lines sink and these are ideal for waggler fishing or legering.

While on the subject of monofilament lines, there have been a number of pre-stretched lines on the market for some time now. It is suggested by the manufacturers that this type of line is stronger than ordinary line, but the elasticity in normal non-stretched lines acts as a buffer if you have to strike hard in order to set the hook home when fishing at a distance.

Reels

Choosing a reel is important. Some anglers purchase a different reel for different jobs, others perhaps only own one, which is used for float fishing and legering. Your choice of reel is equally as important as your choice of a rod, and whilst finance is always a major consideration, it does pay to buy the best reel you can afford. The chances are that if you buy wisely your reel will last for ten or more years.

The American and Japanese manufacturers are now producing reels designed for the British market, many with the increasingly popular skirted spool, a feature which is designed to eliminate the problem of line gathering behind the spool. There are also a number of closed-face reels on the market.

When you buy your first reel, be it for a child, a friend or for yourself, think ahead and buy a reel that will still be useful in a few years time when you or your child have graduated to more sophisticated tackle.

It is of prime importance to fill the spool correctly; some anglers fish with half empty spools, yet in order to cast efficiently, a spool must be filled to capacity. A spool that is not fully filled can restrict your casting ability by as much as 70 per cent. Think of it this way: you have a rod costing perhaps £25, and a reel costing approximately the same, yet you cannot cast 33 yd (30 m) to the fish because you did not spend an extra 80p on the 110 yd (100 m) of line to fill your spool.

Hooks

For float fishing barbless hooks are recommended for two reasons: firstly, they penetrate better and secondly, this applies particularly to the smaller sizes, it is easier to unhook the fish. Among top anglers, there seems to be a trend towards using barbless hooks. This may be influenced by the fact that more patterns are now available than have been in the past.

For legering, particularly when the bait is worm or double maggot, the traditional barbed hook is better. A worm, which tends to be presented

Two spools, much the same, but one will do the job and the other will not. Always fill your spool to its capacity.

stationary for long periods, can wriggle off a barb-less hook, whereas the barb will keep it on.

Hook sizes are largely a question of confidence. Most match anglers are quite happy to fish with tiny hooks, arguing that the smaller the hook the more bites they will get, even if they do lose a few fish. The specimen hunter, on the other hand, uses large hooks, arguing that when he gets a bite, he wants to be sure that the fish is well and truly hooked. It should be the bait that dictates the size of the hook that you use. Obviously a fish hooked on a large hook is less likely to be lost than one on a tiny fine wire hook, but whenever we fish or for whatever species we fish for, bait presentation is the key. There are certain baits which will allow us to use a big hook, bread being a prime example. It is quite easy to bury a size 4 hook into a thumbnail-size piece of flake. Conversely, a single

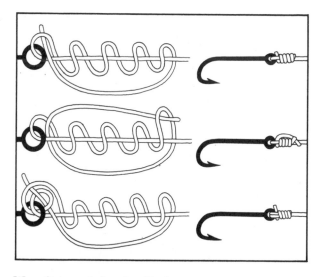

Ways of tying swivels and eyed hooks.

maggot presented on such a hook would look more than a little suspicious. For general fishing you should use either a size 16 hook or a size 18; the size 16 for double maggot and the size 18 for a single maggot.

Balanced tackle
Because no single item is responsible for the capture of fish on its own, it is essential that we fish with balanced tackle; that is each single item of tackle complementing the others. It is pointless using 5 lb (2.25 kg) line in conjunction with a fine tip-actioned match rod. Conversely, it would be equally pointless to use 2 lb (0.90 kg) line in conjunction with a carp rod.

What we first have to establish is what we are fishing for. If your preference is for big fish – carp, barbel, pike and so on – the tackle has to be robust. A 10 or 11 ft (3.05 or 3.35 m) carp rod with a 2 lb (0.90 kg) test curve will serve most purposes. It can be used in conjunction with lines ranging from 4–10 lb (1.80–4.50 kg). If, on the other hand, your preference is for general fishing – roach, bream, chub, perch – a 12 ft (3.65 m) float rod or match rod will be sufficient. But remember that the majority of these rods are designed for use with lines of 2–4 lb (0.90–1.80 kg) breaking strain, 4 lb (1.80 kg) often being the optimum. If heavier lines are used with these rods and a big fish is hooked, there is a chance that in the hands of an inexperienced angler the rod will break before the line.

The key to success is confidence, both in your own ability and your tackle. Tackle does not catch fish, but badly-chosen tackle can prevent you from catching, so understand your tackle and ensure that it is balanced properly.

Baits

There is a seemingly endless number of exotic baits which have accounted for fish over the years. That great angler Richard Walker has caught fish on such varied baits as peas, baked beans, corn-flakes, puffed wheat, earwigs and caterpillars. On that basis it would appear that fish will eat almost anything – and so they will – but not all of the time.

Accepting that whenever we go fishing we are fishing for bites, clearly we must fish with a bait which we know will appeal to the majority of fish. There are exceptions, of course; the specimen hunter who is interested in catching only the bigger specimens will often use a bait which will prove of little interest to the smaller fish such as a potato or a large piece of bread flake.

Maggots
Without doubt, this is the most commonly used bait. They can be used all the year round on both still and moving waters and are available in a variety of colours, red, yellow, white and bronze. In recent years the bronze maggot has proved the most productive. If the maggot has a weakness, it is that small fish have a liking for it; this is not to deny that it will account for the bigger fish if they are present, but small roach, dace and small chub have a tendency to intercept it before it gets down to the bigger fish.

Gozzers

Strictly speaking, the gozzer is the maggot produced by the woodfly, but most people, when talking about gozzers, are referring to a fresh, home-produced maggot. Because of the demand for maggots, it is almost impossible for commercial breeders to produce really fresh ones. Invariably, when an angler buys bait from his local tackle shop, it is at least three or four days old and during that period it will have shrunk and become tough.

Bream are the 'sucker' fish for a really soft white gozzer and as many of our rivers in the east of the country hold big shoals of bream, it is not difficult to understand why the top match anglers go to great lengths to produce a really soft maggot.

Breeding gozzers at home is a simple exercise. Buy a small piece of chicken or lamb's heart, and place it in a biscuit tin or similar container, and lightly cover it with a crumpled newspaper. Place the container under a shed or hedge and leave it. Obviously the breeding of gozzers at home is limited to the summer months, when there is an abundance of flies around, but even during this period it can sometimes take all day for a blow to materialize. When you have succeeded in getting a blow, wrap the meat in two or three sheets of newspaper, put it back in the container and top up with fresh bran (this eliminates the possibility of any odour). Cover the container and place it in the corner of your shed. Now leave it alone; continually opening it will do nothing to enhance the finished gozzer. After seven days, tip the contents on to a riddle and you will find that the gozzers have now come off the feed and should run through quite quickly. Now place the fresh gozzers into a clean container, cover with damp bran and there you have it.

Casters

Since they were first used by the Northern match anglers on the Trent in the late 1960s, casters, which are the chrysalis of the maggot, have become one of the most consistently successful baits around. Every species of coarse fish seems to be vulnerable to a fresh caster, which enjoys the unique distinction of being the only living bait which does not move. Like the maggot, the caster will catch fish throughout the season, but it must be fresh. Casters quickly sour and float, and this can happen in the space of a few hours in high summer. Apart from being a killing bait for big roach and chub, they have now become the accepted feed to use in conjunction with groundbait, when fishing for bream. If you are fishing casters always give them time. They do tend to be slow build-up bait, but once the fish move on to them they seem to like them.

Pinkies

Pink in colour, the pinkie is a small soft maggot, used mostly by canal anglers. You can sometimes catch good quality fish, but they are, in the main, only successful when smaller fish are the quarry – hence their success on canals.

Squatts

A very small maggot, usually used as a feeder, rather than as a hook maggot. They are occasionally used as hookbait in conjunction with tiny 22 or 24 hooks by match anglers, usually when the fishing is hard in the winter.

Worms

Worms, which are a grossly underrated bait, will account for fish even in the worst conditions. They are possibly the best known bait for bream, particularly red worms and lob-worms. Brandlings are popular but they tend to die very quickly. Like maggots, worms can be used all the year round.

Hemp

Used cooked, we do not know why fish, especially roach, should like hemp, but like it they do. It is used mainly as a feed. Roach will sometimes, particularly in the summer months, take it on the hook and when they do, the action is often fast and furious. It is, however, a problem bait, being difficult to keep on the hook. On such occasions tares are a better hookbait.

Tares

Tares, used in conjunction with hemp, can be a devastating hookbait during the warm summer months; but be warned, it is only a summer bait. If you are going to catch on tares you can expect to get a bite fairly quickly. If you have not had a bite after half an hour, it is unlikely that you are going to catch anything on them.

A 5 lb (2.2 kg) tench taken from a Norfolk lake. If this is the type of fish you want to catch, make sure your tackle is up to it: a good Avon-type rod is a must.

Bread

Like worms, bread is a most underrated bait and has possibly accounted for more specimen fish than any other bait. Used as either flake or paste, it tends to work better in clear low water conditions. It can be used all the year round.

Sweetcorn

This is the most devastating bait for specimen fish to have appeared on the angling scene in recent years. Sweetcorn used direct from the tin will sort out the better quality fish, including 20 lb (9 kg) plus carp, 10 lb (4.50 kg) bream and 2 lb (900 g) roach. Apart from match anglers who are always loathe to try new baits, both pleasure anglers and specimen hunters have benefitted from this bait, especially on waters where the bait has been used for some time. Loose fed, like maggots, two grains of corn on a size 10 hook is a killing method. It is most effective in the summer and autumn.

Wasp grub

The largest single problem with wasp grub is acquiring it, but once acquired, it can be a killing bait for chub. It is banned on many waters in the West Midlands, because of its effectiveness. The traditional method of fishing wasp grub is to extract the grubs themselves (they look like very large white maggots). They are very soft, and although they can be made to stay on the hook, many anglers boil them for a couple of minutes before using them. This tends to make them firmer and easier to use. The remains of the cake are then broken up and mixed with groundbait. Another successful method is to fish with the cake on a size 6 or 8 hook. Like tares, wasp grub has its days.

Wheat

This is another summer bait, which should be cooked until it swells and softens. Wheat tends to be at its most effective during July and August. It will account for most species but is generally considered to be a roach bait.

Feeding

It is possibly in the area of feeding that the contrast between the match angler and the novice is most marked. The matchman likes to build his swim slowly, developing it and extracting the maximum amount of fish in his allotted time; increasing and decreasing his rate of feed as fish move in and out of his swim. The novice sits down, throws in some maggots, sometimes a handful, sometimes two handfuls, then stops. Often he will enjoy a flurry of fish, but seldom the consistent catches enjoyed by the more experienced angler.

Feeding, more than any other skill, needs to be mastered if an angler is to put together a large net of fish. He must keep the fish feeding to be in command, because when the fish stop feeding, he will stop catching.

There are two methods of feeding a swim; either by introducing loose feed by hand or catapult, or by groundbaiting. On the right day, either method can be devastating.

Loose feed

Loose feed will usually be hookbait samples, as is the case when we are maggot fishing. However, it is not unusual to fish with a different bait on the hook to that loose fed into the swim, as in the case of hemp and tares or hemp and caster. What we feed is not as important as when and how much. If you are fishing a swim that can be reached by either throwing or catapulting loose feed, it is a better method than groundbaiting. The golden rule is, 'always assume that there are fish in your swim'. You must do this, or you are in trouble because you cannot feed invisible fish.

In a match, where the approximate winning weight is generally known before the start, it is quite easy to decide on a feeding plan, because each angler has a target in mind at the beginning; if the match is going to be won with 10 lb (4.50 kg) of fish, every angler will start feeding with that weight in mind. Obviously not everybody is going to catch 10 lb (4.50 kg) so, as the match develops and the anglers realize that they have not drawn a winning peg, they will cut their feed back and fish for a lower weight in the hope of getting the lower prizes. The situation is different for the pleasure angler because he often does not know the maximum potential of his swim, so he has to decide what weight he is fishing for. Few anglers are likely to catch 40 lb (18 kg) of roach with only 1 pint of maggots, but 4 pt (2.25 litres) maggots thrown in indiscriminately will do nothing to improve the angler's chances of catching in a swim with a potential of only 3–4 lb (1.30–1.80 kg) of fish. So a decision has to be made.

Assuming that an angler decides to float fish a swim that he thinks is capable of producing 10 lb (4.50 kg) of roach, this will probably represent, allowing for the odd 8 oz (225 g) fish, approximately thirty fish. The average fishing session

John Watson with a 20 lb (9 kg) or over mirror carp: taken on luncheon meat at 66 yd (60 m).

lasts five hours, which represents a catch rate of only six fish per hour; not a difficult task, but it can be if the angler throws in a couple of handfuls of maggots at the start. On average, the experts claim that a top class angler will catch 10 per cent of the fish in front of him. Assuming that to be correct, what the angler hopes to do is to excite the fish into feeding by making them compete for his loose offerings. The secret is not to throw in too much feed, because this creates a situation whereby the fish can feed at their leisure. If the angler starts by feeding twenty or thirty maggots every cast, he should start to get bites pretty quickly provided that his hookbait is being presented well. The secret now is to keep the bites coming.

Throughout the day there will be a turnover of fish in the swim. An angler might start off catching roach in the 2–3 oz (55–85 g) class, then the swim will die. They may then catch fish in the 4–6 oz (115–170 g) class. What happens is that when a shoal of better fish move into your swim, the smaller fish move out. What the angler must be prepared to do is to adjust both his hook presentation and his feeding pattern when this happens.

It is an acknowledged fact that it is more difficult to fish efficiently in rivers than on stillwaters. However, in the area of feeding, the situation is reversed. The river angler can over-feed his swim, but because that feed is being carried away by the current, no lasting harm is done, unless of course he continues to over-feed. The stillwater angler does not enjoy such an advantage. Whatever feed he puts in stays on the bottom. Consequently, if he has fed in 200 maggots at the start and there are only 100 fish in front of him, it is going to be pure good fortune if one of the fish picks up his hookbait. Furthermore, because of the abundance of food which is now lying on the bottom, a number of fish will become well fed within a short space of time and instead of having 100 feeding fish in front of him the angler could, within the space of ten to fifteen minutes, have reduced this to sixty or even less. By introducing another large handful of maggots this number can quickly be reduced even further and rather than developing the swim, slowly building it up, so that the maximum number of fish can be caught, the swim will have

A 4 lb (1.8 kg) bream being netted. On this occasion the angler had to wait one and a half hours for his first bite, but he had fed enough to enable him to catch another five without feeding again.

been destroyed by indiscriminate feeding.

Always start slowly, introducing only ten to twenty maggots at a time. If the fish are there, you will begin to get bites. The secret is to feed every cast, so that your hookbait is falling through the water with your loose feed. If you find that the fish are coming off the bottom and taking your bait 'on the drop', adjust your shotting accordingly. However, if you find that only the smaller fish are coming up in the water while the better fish continue feeding on the bottom, step up your feed, because much of what you are putting in is not reaching the bottom, it is being intercepted by the smaller fish in mid-water. If you do not get food to the better fish, they will move, especially if they are in the mood to feed.

Sometimes you have a situation where small fish are feeding in mid-water, and you are after the larger ones on the bottom. If, on the way down, your float dips but a proper bite does not manifest itself, always reel in and check your maggot; nine times out of ten you will find the end nipped. You will seldom get a bite once your maggot has burst, so there seems little point in sitting ten minutes waiting for a bite which is not going to come, when it takes only seconds to change a maggot and re-cast.

One often reads that the best method of loose feeding is 'little and often', but it is an ambiguous statement. 'A little and often' on fast-flowing rivers like the Trent or the Severn constitutes throwing in much more feed than on a stillwater or a canal, because you are casting and feeding more often. To be more precise; you should feed for one fish at a time; once you have caught it, fish for your next one. By doing this, you will not make the mistake of throwing feed in indiscriminately – a root cause of many spoilt swims.

Groundbait

It is important to define exactly what good groundbait is, because much of what is sold in tackle shops is anything but good. The best groundbait is finely-ground breadcrumb; not biscuit or rusk, just plain bread. When mixed it should be fluffy, not stodgy, and it should cloud as it strikes the surface of the water. It should not be mixed with additives like meat or fish, because they do not fulfil the function that groundbait should perform.

Groundbait is used under the following circumstances: fishing at distance, beyond the range of your loose feed catapult, and when fishing for bream. There are other occasions of course, for example, on deep rivers. What many novice anglers fail to realize is that groundbait is used by the experienced angler as a carrier and not as a feed.

We do not know why bream respond so well to groundbait, but of all the coarse fish they are the one species that responds best to this method of feeding. Although they can be caught with loose feed, they are by nature a nervous fish, seldom caught close in, but, preferring to roam 33–44 yd (30–40 m) from the bank. Because bream are a nervous fish, feeding correctly is crucial. The most difficult situation you can encounter when bream fishing, is to start fishing with the shoal already in front of you. Do you feed and possibly frighten them away, or fish without feeding, in which case they will drift away, possibly to the next angler on the bank? In all honesty there is no answer to that one. All you can do is mix your groundbait as wet as possible so that it goes in with the minimum amount of disturbance.

Accepting that groundbait in itself is not adequate feed to stop a patrolling shoal of bream, what we want is a mixture of feed and groundbait that, upon impact with the water, will cloud and fall to the bottom to create a carpet of feed, which will prove attractive to the fish. What we do not want is a series of little mounds, which is what happens when groundbait is incorrectly mixed. The correct utensil for mixing groundbait is a shallow wide-topped bowl, not a bucket. If you add water to a bucket of groundbait, the outcome is wet, sloppy groundbait on the top and dry groundbait on the bottom. Always put the water in the bowl first then add the groundbait. The reason for this being that by adding the groundbait to the water you ensure that it is all dampened evenly. Having done that, you should have a nice fluffy texture, not a stodgy mess. Now add your feed. As a rule of thumb, add 1 pt (500 ml) of casters or squatts to every pound of groundbait. That may sound a lot, but because groundbait is inexpensive compared to casters or maggots, anglers invariably mix too much. Never mix maggots with groundbait, because they can break up the ball in the air, and because, as it is possible to wait for up to an hour for a bite, you can never be sure that they will remain lying on top of the groundbait, whereas casters do not move.

If you have mixed your groundbait properly, so that it breaks into a cloud upon contact with the water, the effect when it reaches the bottom will be of casters nestling on a fine bed of groundbait. If, on the other hand, you have mixed a bowl of stodgy groundbait, the outcome will be that the ball will not break up until it reaches the bed of the lake or river, and will leave little lumps of feed here and there. Instead of the casters alone being totally irresistible, the stodge with casters embedded becomes attractive to the fish. If your caster hookbait is nearby it will probably be taken by the fish, but you are filling the fish up with stodge at the same time. Remember that you want to feed them, but not fill them.

Try to get your feed in before the bream move into your swim. Sometimes you have to put feed on top of a shoal of feeding bream and they do not always seem to mind, but it is the exception rather than the rule. Having chosen your swim, open up with three balls the size of tennis balls, laced, with either squatts or casters. Then be governed by what you hope to catch, and where the fish are. If you only expect to catch two or three fish, add another two balls at the off and leave it at that. If you are hoping to put a weight together, after your initial three balls, do nothing for fifteen minutes, other than watch for signs, line bites and so on. If there are none, feed at regular intervals, until either you see indications of fish being there, or the anglers on either side of you catch a bream. By that time, you should have enough feed in your swim to hold them.

Five match anglers with a combined catch of over 200 lb (90 kg). The result of careful feeding.

Chapter 2
The coarse fish

Big fish angler Steve Harper poses with a super 11 lb 14 oz
(5.3 kg) barbel from the fast-flowing River Wensum.

Barbel

Found mainly in fast streamy rivers, like the Hampshire Avon, the Dorset Stour, the Severn, and latterly the Trent and its tributaries, the barbel is, for its weight, one of the hardest fighting species.

Often growing in excess of 10 lb (4.50 kg), the torpedo shape of the barbel and its ability to hug the bottom makes it a very sporting fish. With its underslung mouth, it is very much a bottom feeder, and it will take all manner of different baits; maggots, casters, luncheon meat, hemp, bread and worms have all accounted for this species.

Until ten years ago the Hampshire Avon and the Dorset Stour were the rivers normally associated with this species, but since their introduction into the River Severn in the mid-1960s, they have spread and multiplied to such a degree that they can now be caught almost throughout the river. Certainly, fish have been taken as far downstream as Tewkesbury, with catches even in matches exceeding 100 lb (450 kg) during the summer months.

Although barbel can be caught by most known methods, in recent years the swim-feeder/maggot combination has proved to be the most effective, especially on the Severn and the Trent. The use of maggots is barred during the summer months on a number of stretches of the Stour and Hampshire Avon, so the traditional methods of legered luncheon meat, hemp, bread and worms are practised most on these venues.

It is possible to catch a fish without putting in any feed at all, other than that which is on the hook, but that is merely to 'chuck it and chance it', unless of course you are casting to a particular fish. Because the angler is limited to the amount of time which he can spend at the water's edge, it is not unreasonable that he should want to catch as many fish as possible whilst he is there. The problem is, how do you concentrate your feed into a small area on a river that is running hard? The answer is, by using the blockend swimfeeder.

Prior to the summer of 1975 it was not unusual to hear of matches being won on the Severn with 35 lb (15.80 kg) of chub and barbel; this weight would invariably have been taken on the float. But in 1975 the match anglers discovered the swimfeeder and immediately weights rocketed, with as many as twenty anglers catching in excess of 60 lb (27.20 kg) of barbel in a single match. Quite simply, a large blockend feeder filled to capacity was cast into the fast streamy waters. Provided that it was cast to roughly the same spot each time, a steady build-up of feed began to emerge, as each cast deposited more maggots in the swim. Barbel are very much a shoaling fish, especially in the 2–4 lb (900 g–1.8 kg) bracket, the result being that loose-fed maggots, which were used previously, would be carried downstream by the flow, spreading the shoal. The opposite happened with the feeder; the maggots were deposited in a small area on the bottom, and consequently the shoal was kept very tight.

Barbel are very much a summer species, although they can be caught throughout the year. However, as the year wears on and the first frosts of winter send the water temperature down, the massive bags which can be expected in July and August begin to diminish. Because of their preference for fast water, barbel are used to taking food at speed. In fact, barbel tend to intercept a bait then turn with it; this accounts for their habit of almost pulling the rod off its rest. What happens is that as the fish picks up the bait and turns, the weight of the feeder is sufficient to set the hook; the hooked fish then tears off upstream. When this happens, there is no need to strike because the hook is already set. As the winter wears on and the water gets colder, the fish are reluctant to move quite so much and bites become more finicky, so you do not need to use so much bait. As a rule of thumb, use as much as 1 gal (4.50 litres) of maggots on a summer outing, but only 2 pt (1 litre) in the winter. The fish are not as tightly shoaled in the winter months, nor do they feed so actively.

Bronze bream

Unlike barbel, bream are seldom found in hard-running water; they prefer slow-moving or still-water. They are a shoaling fish and can be the easiest of all the coarse fish to catch when they are in the mood to feed, but they can also be the most elusive.

Because of their shape – they tend to be plate-shaped – they are not fierce fighters; expect a slow dogged fight rather than the violent surges of a chub. It is the pursuit of bream that makes them exciting and they are seldom caught by accident in lakes or rivers. Because of their cautious nature they prefer the security of the deeper water often found well away from the bank and for this reason, the angler who wishes to catch bream must often fish for them to the exclusion of other fish.

Bream are patrolling fish. Often they will be seen rolling in one part of a lake, only to be seen an hour later 110 yd (100 m) further on. However, their movements are not indiscriminate; careful observation will show that they tend to follow the same patrol routes each day, and if bream are to be caught in any quantity, this factor must be recognized.

If you are going to fish for bream, location is the key. Unlike other species, bream can be observed because they tend to roll on the surface. Why they do this we do not know, for there is little to suggest they are surface feeders. If you decide to fish for bream, try to spend some time locating the patrol route; the best time is in the evening when the water is flat. Bear in mind also that it is possible that, as the day wears on, the fish will venture nearer to the bank, and it will be much easier to fish and feed at 27 yd (25 m) than it is at 66 yd (60 m).

If you do observe bream in a particular spot in the evening, it is unlikely that you will catch them there at other times of the day.

The secret with bream fishing, accepting that fish will, during the course of the day, pass through your swim, is to ensure that you have enough feed on the bottom to stop the shoal as they pass; one ball of groundbait or a swimfeeder won't hold thirty or forty fish for very long.

Correct groundbaiting for bream is possibly the most crucial factor in their capture, an ill-timed ball or the use of poor groundbait can spell disaster.

Since the development of the swingtip and latterly the quiver and springtip, bite indication on legered baits has improved out of all recognition. Many specimen anglers still insist on using dough-bobbins and such like, but quite frankly they are being short-sighted in trying to hold on to a tradition and a method which is inefficient and out-dated. The spring quiver is without doubt the most efficient stillwater bite indicator on the market today. On slow-moving water the quivertip is unbeatable.

Bream, whilst appearing to prefer a stationary bait will, and again this demonstrates their unpredictability, sometimes take a moving bait. Then the big float is called for. This to my mind is bream fishing at its most exciting; legering is fun, but having put in your feed and cast out, it's very often a question of patience. With the float, much more skill is required, especially if the fish are 25–30 yd (23–27 m) out from the bank.

Reel line of 2.6 or 3 lb (1.20 or 1.40 kg) is needed with a 1.7 lb (0.77 kg) hook length and a bodied waggler carrying 3 swan shot. Most of the shot is placed immediately around the float to give the maximum casting distance. One method is to use a No. 10 shot 9 in (22 cm) from the hook, which will drag over the bottom and steady the bait; 18 in (45 cm) above that, a No. 8 shot and 24 in (60 cm) above that two No. 6 shot: then cast out beyond the baited area. This has a double effect; firstly, the float is not landing directly on top of feeding fish; and secondly it is possible, by merely dropping the rod end into the water, to reel the float back to the baited area, sinking the line in the process. When you are fishing at this distance it is crucial that you do this, as a bow quickly develops, dragging your float away from the baited area.

Like barbel, bream are predominantly a summer species. They will take most baits, including maggots, casters, worms and bread, although bread seems to be at its most effective during the early part of the season. If you can catch them in the right mood it is possible to catch a netful, but you could return to the same spot the very next day and never get a bite.

Carp

There are four main species of carp found in our water. Crucian carp attract very little real attention, although they are great fun to catch, but grow only to 2 lb (900 g) or 3 lb (1.30 kg). The mirror carp, leather carp and common carp, on the other hand, attain enormous proportions, with fish in excess of 30 lb (13.50 kg) being caught each year.

Since the capture of the record carp by Richard Walker in 1952, something of a cult following has sprung up around the species, with secret baits being developed by anglers fishing on secret waters. There are some club-controlled waters which contain large species of carp, but these are few and far between. Most waters containing big carp, this is fish in excess of 10 lb (4.50 kg), tend to be controlled by private syndicates.

The attraction of carp with their thick-set bronzed body is that they are spectacular fighters. Even the smaller 4–6 lb (1.8–3 kg) fish will often offer tremendous sport to the angler fishing with light line. They are also a highly intelligent fish and because of this carp baits have been developed to a most sophisticated level, with high proteins and amino acids being used. In fact certain baits that are now being used by anglers are required to be taken to the water's edge in an ice-box, but this is generally on waters that contain very large fish which have been caught before. On waters that contain smaller fish, most baits are acceptable: maggots, worms, casters, bread and in recent times sweetcorn, which has possibly accounted for more specimen fish than any other bait and certainly carp to 20lb (9kg) have been taken. It is perhaps fair to say that it is losing some of its seemingly magical appeal now, but it is nevertheless still a marvellous bait, being easy to use and cheap to purchase.

The average angler is likely to encounter fish in the 4–10lb (1.80–4.50kg) bracket. If you plan to fish for carp, ensure that you tackle up with the proper equipment. Most reputable companies manufacture a good range of carp rods, which are suitable for catching fish up to 10lb (4.50kg). If, however, you feel that you wish to specialize, it is worth purchasing a rod from one of the companies making rods for the big fish specialists. It is possible that you will pay a little more for your rod, but, when the opportunity arises to fish for a really big specimen, your tackle will be up to the job.

Two or three fish in the 10lb (4.50kg) category would represent a good day's fishing, therefore your feeding pattern must be different from the 'little and often' type used for roach and chub fishing. With the exception of the River Trent, there are very few rivers which offer the carp angler the promise of any real sport. Accepting that most carp fishing is restricted to stillwaters, remember that whatever feed is put into a lake stays in the lake, so ensure that the swim is fed correctly.

Because carp is a larger and, there is much evidence to show, more intelligent fish, bait presentation is crucial, so always ensure that the bait

Shotting pattern for bream fishing.

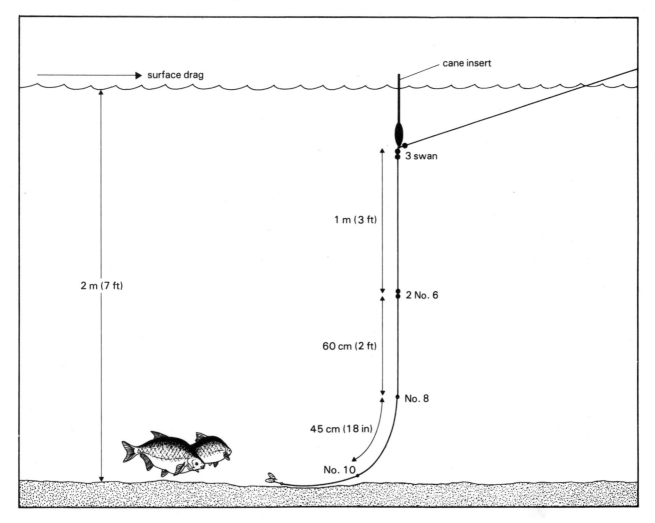

you are using dictates the size of hook you use. You are still fishing for bites, because if you don't get a bite you cannot catch a fish. If you are using maggots, don't try to get eight on a size 10 hook, just because that's the hook you were using with another bait; maggots don't crawl around the bottom in eights. When a carp moves into a swim baited with either maggots or sweetcorn, the bait will by lying perfectly naturally on the bottom. If they are cautious of that particular bait, they are far more likely to be suspicious of a great clump of maggots than they are of one or two, so try to make your hookbait as inconspicuous as possible.

The same applies to line: 4 or 5lb (1.80 or 2.25 kg) breaking strain line will cope with any fish up to 10lb (4.50 kg), provided that there are no snags in the swim you are fishing. Don't be stereotyped; many anglers fish with 6lb (2.70 kg) line regardless of the swim. Always fish as fine a line as possible, without being reckless. Fine line is more subtle than thick line; fish often suck a bait into their mouths from 4–5in (10–12 cm) away, and two maggots on a size 16 hook to 3lb (1.35 kg) line will move much more naturally than eight maggots on 10 to 8lb (3.50 kg) line.

Chub

Although chub have been introduced quite successfully into a number of stillwaters they are fundamentally a river fish, but unlike other species which tend to colonize in certain types of water, chub can be found in all types of water from the fast-flowing Hampshire Avon to the virtually still River Welland. They abound in small streams but are equally at home on big rivers like the Trent and the Wye. But whenever you fish for chub there is one thing you can be certain of, if there is a snag or fallen tree in the water, there will be chub close by.

The great beauty of this species is that they will feed throughout the year, falling to maggots, casters, hemp, worms, bread, crayfish, wasp grub, snails, cheese and slugs, fished on almost any method, float, leger, swimfeeder or freelined. However, having said that, they can also be most elusive, particularly the bigger specimens.

If your thoughts are on catching big chub, stout tackle is the order of the day; an Avon-type rod and 4 or 5lb (1.80 or 2.25 kg) line are advisable. Small chub are a shoaling fish, and those in the 1–2lb (450–900 g) class can offer great sport when fished for on match tackle; maggots and casters

are generally the most productive bait for this type of fishing.

Dace

Dace are often mistaken for small chub and whilst it is possible to identify them by their concave fins (chub have convex fins) dace tend to have a much smaller mouth than chub of a similar size. Found in fast running waters, dace are a fun fish. A dace weighing 1 lb (450 g) is in fact a specimen-sized fish but it is quantity rather than quality that counts with this species. Locate a shoal, loose feed maggots and the sport is fast and furious on float-fished tackle. Because of their size, small baits like bread punch, casters and maggots are the most productive bait.

They are winter fish and will feed in the coldest weather. Fine tackle is the order of the day; a match rod 2lb (0.90 kg) line and small hooks, size 16 or 18.

Eel

A much maligned species of fish that will feed on almost anything, small eels can be found in almost all of our rivers and many stillwaters.

Like chub, eels are great lovers of snags, and because of this you will need stout tackle when you are fishing for them. A pike rod is ideal, line of 8–10lb (3.50–4.50 kg) is advisable, with bunches of worms fished on a size 6 or 8 hook being the most productive bait. For the larger species (5lb: 2.20 kg) location is the key, for not all lakes that hold small eels necessarily hold large ones. Many living in rivers return to the Sargasso Sea before they attain large proportions, and while a number may remain in the river it is impossible to fish with a bait that will attract 5lb (2.20 kg) fish and not 2lb (900 g) ones. Therefore it is important, if you wish to catch large eels, that you establish that such fish exist in the waters which you are fishing.

For large eels, dead baits have proved a most successful method, but remember that unlike other predators, eels have a comparitively small mouth, so portions of fish, rather than whole fish tend to be more successful. Much has been written about when is the best time to strike when using dead baits.

Carp.

Chub.

Gudgeon

The canal angler's friend, gudgeon live in all types of water, but seem to be most prolific in the canals. Weighing only a few ounces, gudgeon offer little in the way of real sport except for the canal match angler, who is content to fish for them during the winter months, when as little as 1 lb (450 g) of fish can win a match.

Because of their size, gudgeon are best fished for on fine tackle, small hooks size 18 or 20 and small baits, such as maggots, pinkies and squatts.

Perch

This was once one of the most popular species of fish in our waters, but since the perch disease began to take its toll in the early 1970s we have seen an alarming decline in this delightful species.

Perch are predators and can be caught throughout the year. They will respond to all manner of methods: dead bait, live bait, float fishing and legering. Small perch can be caught on the crudest of tackle, but as they grow, they become harder to catch.

A 12 ft or 13 ft (3.65 m or 3.95 m) float rod and 2½ lb (1.10 kg) line are adequate to deal with most perch, although fish in the 3–4 lb (1.30–1.80 kg) class will call for sturdier tackle. Worm is a favourite bait, although caster and maggot can be killing baits.

Pike

The pike, with its long, tapered body, is built for speed, and it is the largest of all the predatory fish to inhabit our waters. Pike can be found in every river and most lakes and ponds. It is a much maligned species that many anglers, quite wrongly, blame for the decline of fisheries. In reality, this is seldom the case. In fact, the presence of pike often makes for a better fishery because they will eat dead and diseased fish.

The pike angler seldom expects to catch anything other than pike, except in the Fenland area where the recently introduced zander will respond to similar methods. It is very much specialist fishing, and is dealt with in detail in Chapter 4.

Roach

This delightful fish is the most common and most fished for species in our waters. They respond best

to a float-fished bait although many specimen-sized fish are caught on legered bread. They are a shoaling fish that can offer a good day's fishing, and which fight well. They can be persuaded to feed on the coldest of days.

Light match tackle is most suitable for roach fishing. Line of 2 lb (0.90 kg), stick float or waggler, light shotting, small hooks, size 16 or 18, and loose-fed casters or maggots will generally bring them on to feed especially as the year wears on. They are at their best during the months of September and October, but they will feed throughout the winter.

Rudd

Rudd are widespread, but are not often fished for because of their nomadic tendencies. They seldom feed on the bottom and are generally caught on the drop or in mid-water. The problem is that they will seldom settle in an area long enough for anglers to catch many. They are often found living in or around weed beds. As in roach fishing, light tackle is called for if the best results are to be achieved; a very lightly shotted float should be ideal.

Tench

Of all the coarse fish, the tench is perhaps the one for which all anglers feel a great affection. It is a very beautiful fish, with its smooth olive green scales, its large fins and small red eyes. Seldom caught during the winter months, tench abound in the summer, when the water temperature is at its highest.

Traditionally associated with stillwaters, tench thrive quite happily in most of our rivers, but it is in lakes and ponds that they are mainly pursued.

For many years, in fact until the early 1970s, a 6 lb (2.70 kg) tench was looked upon as massive, but then, for no explainable reason, many of the specialist tench anglers began catching tench of 7–8 lb (3.10–3.60 kg) and even the odd 9 lb (4 kg) fish, and then in 1975, a fish of 10 lb 1 oz 2 drm (4 kg 567 g) was taken: a new British record.

The cause of this sudden appearance of large tench has been the subject of much debate. Could it be that fish of that size have always been present, but anglers were unable to catch them? There is some evidence to suggest that this may be a possibility.

Like bream, tench are a wandering fish, but

rather than seeking the deep water away from the water's edge, they love to forage in the marginal weed which abounds during the summer months. They are a bottom feeder, and tend to feed rather like the action of a vacuum cleaner, sucking in alga and insects off the bottom, eating that which they desire and blowing out that which they do not.

Although it is possible to catch tench throughout the day there does seem to be a marked increase in their desire to feed both early in the morning around dawn and late in the evening. Like carp, they will feed on most baits, but they have in recent years shown a distinct liking for sweetcorn; and bread is also a favourite bait.

Because tench show a liking for weeds, stout tackle is called for, in the form of a powerful rod and line to suit the occasion. They are strong fighting fish, and seldom come to the net easily.

Zander

The first zander were introduced into the land-locked Woburn Abbey lake in 1878, but they did not at that time seem to acclimatize particularly well to our water. In 1963, ninety-seven fingerlings were introduced into the Great Ouse Relief Channel and were thus given the opportunity of escaping from man's control. The spread of zander has been prolific. So much so, that it is claimed that they have in their search for food wiped out complete fisheries in the East Anglian region.

Unlike pike, zander are shoaling fish that hunt in packs. They show a preference for small fish, tearing into shoals of skimmer bream. Most anglers fishing for zander in East Anglia tend to employ similar tactics to those when pike fishing, scaling down both hooks and bait size.

Tench.

An angler float fishing Ireland's River Erne.

Chapter 3
Fishing methods

Floatfishing

Of all the methods at the angler's disposal, the one that gives the most satisfaction and requires the most skill is float fishing. Unlike legering or swim-feeder fishing, where the bait is stationary, the moving bait needs to be controlled if it is to be effective. The stick float and waggler are often fished on gossamer-thin monofilament line, and in the hands of a novice can be a nightmare, but in the hands of the expert they can yield fish after fish.

If you want to improve you floatfishing techniques it is as crucial, first of all, that you understand what is in your float box: why an inserted waggler will work one day and not the next; when to fish with shot strung out on the line, and when to bunch it; what the difference is between a peacock insert and a cane insert.

There are two types of float: those which are attached to the line top and bottom, called stick floats and balsas; and those which are fixed through the bottom eye only called wagglers. In a nutshell, floats fixed top and bottom are for use on moving waters only; wagglers, on the other hand, can be used on still and slow-moving waters.

Because anglers are compulsive purchasers of floats, they invariably carry too many, most of which they never use. Let us look at what we should carry in our float boxes, and why.

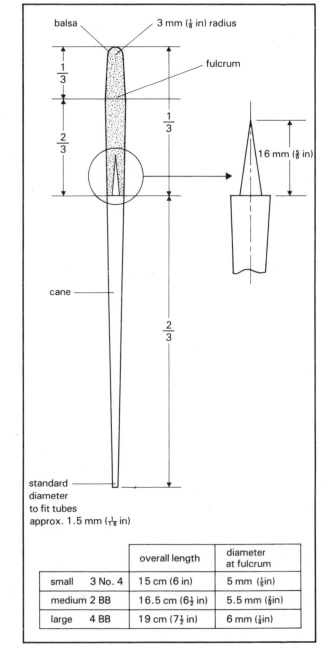

The construction of a stick float. All stick floats should meet these specifications. The shot capacity can vary fractionally on these dimensions to the density of balsa wood.

		overall length	diameter at fulcrum
small	3 No. 4	15 cm (6 in)	5 mm ($\frac{1}{5}$ in)
medium	2 BB	16.5 cm (6$\frac{1}{2}$ in)	5.5 mm ($\frac{2}{5}$ in)
large	4 BB	19 cm (7$\frac{1}{2}$ in)	6 mm ($\frac{1}{4}$ in)

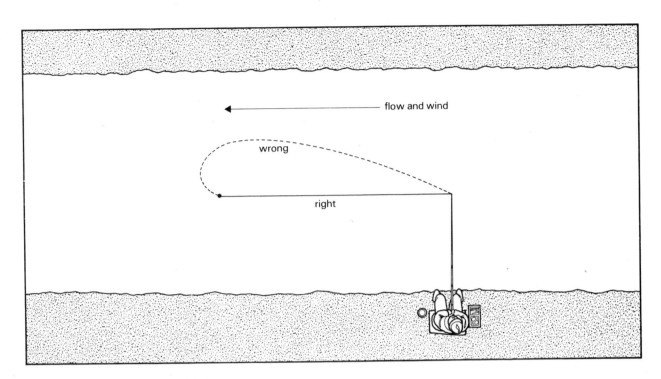

It is important to keep the line behind the float.

Basic stick float set-up.

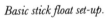

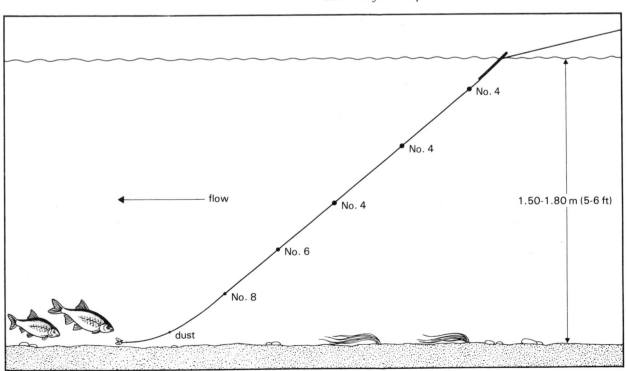

The stick float

This is the most limited, yet the most important, float, the better ones are those bearing the following names: Clive Smith, Kenny Giles, Max Winters, Pete Warren or Ultra. There are others, but the five mentioned produce good floats consistently.

The stick float is the only float over which the angler has complete control in moving water. It is limited because in depths of over 10 ft (3 m) or when fished more than two or three rod lengths from the bank, control is often lost and the waggler begins to come into its own.

Wind dictates how efficiently the stick can be fished. Ideally, the float should be fished over depths and eased gently down the swim, keeping the line between rod tip and float behind the float at all times. This becomes difficult when you are confronted with either a facing or a downstream wind. The most favourable wind is upstream and coming off your shoulder, because it allows you to hold the line off the water, controlling the float down your swim.

A selection of stick and balsa floats.

Because fish are invariably caught very close when stick float fishing, it is important that floating lines like Beyer or Racine Tortue are used, so that the strike is clean and quiet. Old or sinking lines tend to cause unnecessary disturbance.

Shotting is crucial, but sadly there are few hard and fast rules to help the novice, because depth and flow dictate what shot goes on the line. A simple guideline is: always ensure that your shots decrease in size the nearer they are to the hook.

Two further points to remember are that, unless you are experienced, never try to fish a stick in a downstream wind; and never try to fish further out than you can cast underarm as you will lose control of the float.

Balsas

Balsas are the most straightforward float, being made entirely of balsa wood. Like the stick float, they are fished top and bottom. They are made for use in fast streamy rivers like the Wye or the Ribble.

Waggler

The waggler is a type of float, that is fished loose, locked on to the line with a shot either side of the

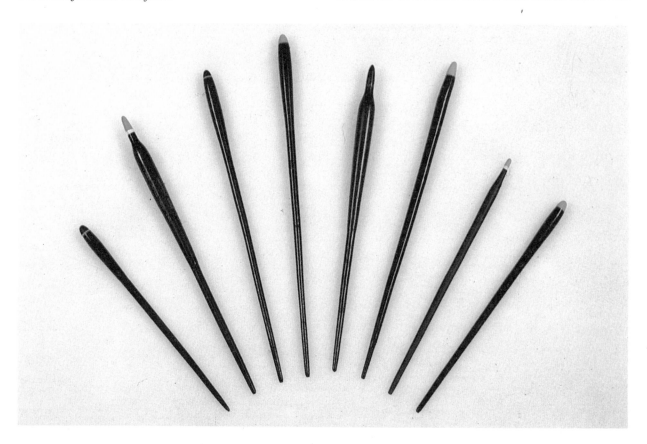

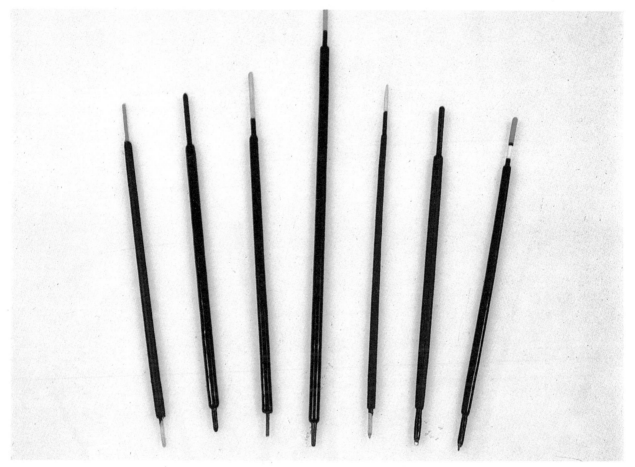

A set of straight sarkandas and peacock wagglers.

eye. Into this category fall missiles, antennas and duckers and the main advantage that these floats have over stick floats is that they can be fished at a distance. The principal ingredients in the manufacture of wagglers is peacock quill or sarkandas reed.

The advantage of waggler floats is that they can be cast considerable distances: the disadvantage is that the angler has very little real control over the float, apart from mending line, as the float fishes itself, running through the swim at the speed of the current. It cannot be held back or eased down, as can the stick. Wagglers are available in a great variety of sizes, from those taking two No. 1 shot to the large-bodied types taking as much as four swan shot. It is with the bigger floats that most inexperienced anglers get into trouble, because they tend to become confused as how best to locate so much shot on the line. As with the stick float, there are no hard and fast rules about shotting, but remember that, because the waggler is fished loose, it cannot be fished in turbulent water; consequently, the need for a necklace of shot on the line is eliminated.

Shotting

In the past anglers have created all manner of fancy shotting patterns. Nowadays, however, match anglers are much more sensible in their approach. The basic shotting pattern is as follows: the bulk of the shot is placed directly underneath the float with perhaps two No. 4s 4ft (1.20m) from the hook, two No. 6s below that, followed by a single No. 6 and a No. 8 1ft (30cm) from the hook. In deep water over 9ft (2.70m), place two No. 1s at mid-depth, to get the bait down quicker. If you are fishing overdepth, include a No. 10 shot on the hook length, allowing this to drag the bottom, which will have the effect of steadying up the hookbait. A special shotting pattern for bream is given in Chapter 2.

It is difficult to write about shotting because conditions dictate what goes on the line, and conditions change constantly. So much so, in fact, that it is not uncommon to change a float or a shotting pattern five or six times during the course

A selection of bodied wagglers.

of a five-hour match. Accepting that that can happen on a single peg in such a short period of time, it is impossible to describe a shotting pattern which will work on all manner of waters. Think about the shot that you put on the line; ask yourself, 'Why am I putting that shot there?' If you cannot answer that question, take it off.

Choice of waggler

Many anglers fail to relate what they are trying to achieve with the float they are using. Choice of float is dictated by the position of the fish (how far out), depth, wind and flow. If, on a stillwater, the surface water is moving in the opposite direction to the natural drift, a float that is long enough to get under the surface drift is called for; if bites are shy, a cane or reed insert is called for. Waggler fishing is easy if you think about the job in hand.

There are a number of floats which, whilst in essence being wagglers, have at some time been designed to fulfil a specific function and consequently have a special name. The missile, for example, is a large-bodied waggler loaded with a brass insert. The zoomer is another loaded-bodied waggler. It is probably the only waggler float that is fished top and bottom. However, it is seldom used these days. The ducker is simply a bodied waggler. Try not to fall into the trap of having favourite floats: keep an open mind and always choose the float which is best suited to the conditions at the time.

Legering

Legering is a method of fishing with a lead weight anchored firmly on the bottom. It is not in itself a recently devised method; in fact, there is evidence to suggest that this form of fishing was practised in the days of Izaak Walton. Until quite recently, however, the fundamental problem with the method was one of bite detection. Bites were signalled either by the fish bolting and pulling the end of the angler's rod, or by the angler holding his line gently between his fingers and feeling for a biting fish (a method still employed today by certain specimen hunters). In 1957, a tackle dealer by the name of Jack Clayton devised the first swingtip, and whilst few people took the swingtip seriously in the beginning, this method was to revolutionize legering within a few years.

Legering has many advantages, the most important being that it allows the angler to perform two functions which cannot be performed on the float: to fish efficiently at a great distance (up to 88 yd/80 m from the bank); and to present a still bait in moving water. These are two major advantages when fishing large reservoirs or rivers like the Welland and the Great Ouse.

By today's standards the early swingtip was crude, but with the tremendous growth of match fishing, legering has been developed to a more sophisticated level, with anglers like Ivan Marks, Johnny Hart and Freddie Foster adding much to its improvement. Today, it is not unusual to see anglers fishing with 7 ft (2 m) hook lengths and tiny size 20 hooks and catching bream 'on the drop'. But like so many aspects of fishing, it is the few top anglers who are getting the maximum results from the method.

As rivers become more polluted and the price of petrol remains high, anglers are looking to fish closer to home. This often means going to the local reservoir or gravel pit, and nowhere can legering be more successful than on this type of venue. Invariably the waters are popular with anglers, particularly if they hold a good head of fish. At the weekend, every peg is taken and bankside disturbance is considerable, causing the fish to move from the margins to the sanctuary of the deeper water, often 33–44 yd (30–40 m) from the bankside. Whilst it is possible for the experienced angler to fish efficiently at this distance using a float, it is a situation that really calls for the leger, especially if the quarry is bream, for no species of fish responds better to a well-presented stationary bait than this one.

The set-up

When legering, the rod will, for the most part, be positioned on a rod rest, so a 9 or 10 ft (2.75 or 3.05 m) rod is ideal. The rod should be through-actioned, allowing the angler to use fine line 2 lb (0.90 kg) if he wishes; the bite indicator can be a swingtip, quivertip or springtip.

If conditions are good and there is not too much tow on the water a springtip is best because it offers no resistance to a biting fish, whereas the swingtip and the quivertip offer an increasing amount of resistance the further they are pulled.

If the conditions are poor, with wind and broken water, try using a quivertip and target board combination. The target is a black board approximately 9 in (22 cm) square with a 3 in (7 cm) white band painted down the middle. It is fixed to a bank stick and positioned 12 in (30 cm) from the end of the rod, so that when the rod is

Fishing with a swingtip. Note how the rod is set at a 45° angle to the bank, giving the angler the best view of his tip.

positioned on the rest, the quivertip shows up clearly against the white background. This helps considerably when the tip is being moved by high winds or waves.

If conditions are good and you are not planning to fish in excess of 50 yd (45 m) out, and you are expecting to catch a good bag of fish, you could use a swingtip. When, for example, a big bag of bream can be put together, a large number of line bites will be experienced. When using a springtip, which is extremely sensitive, it is very difficult to tell the difference between the real bites and the line bites. And bearing in mind how easy it is to scare bream, you want to avoid striking at false bites as this drags the bomb across the backs of the feeding fish.

Line of 3 lb (1.35 kg) will handle most fish, as long as the lake or reservoir is fairly snag-free.

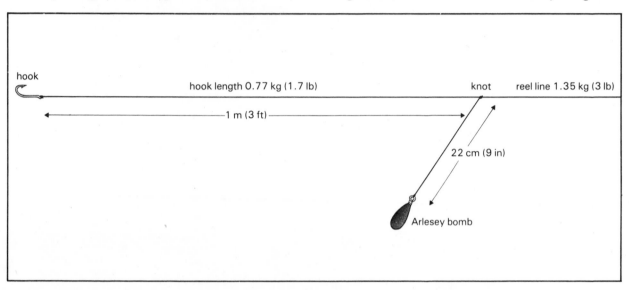

Paternoster rig. For feeder fishing, replace the bomb with a feeder.

Using a sliding link.

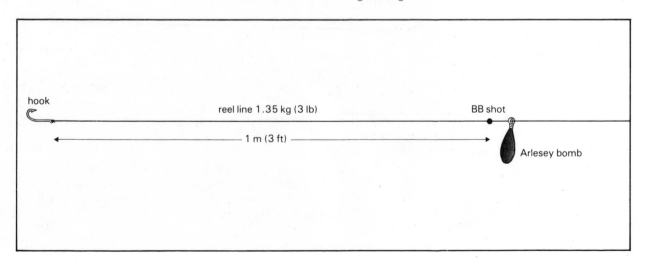

The quivertip and target board set-up. The parallel lines on the target board will show the angler any movement which his tip might make. Also, the rod tip is seen very clearly because it is viewed against a dark background.

However, some people prefer to use slightly heavier line. A good, open-faced, fixed spool reel is best. On days when there is little or no wind, it is a good policy to 'feather' the line as your bomb hits the water, causing the minimum amount of splash. It is much easier to do this with an open-faced reel than a closed-face one.

Arlesey bombs and hook sizes are determined by the bait used and the distance fished. Bread flake, for example, is very wind resistant; a ⅜oz (10g) bomb will carry a maggot or worm bait 44–55yd (40–50m) with ease under normal conditions, yet a ½oz (15g) Arlesey bomb is needed to carry a piece of bread flake the same distance. Hook sizes are determined by the bait used, for bread a size 6 or 8; for maggots a size 16 or 18; and for worm a size 12 or 14. Many anglers make the mistake of allowing the hook to dictate the bait, which is shortsighted because it is the bait that catches the fish, not the hook.

Terminal rigs

Much has been written about terminal rigs in recent years. Without doubt, the most efficient terminal rig for *all* leger fishing is the fixed paternoster. The length of line between bomb and hook is variable, but normally a 3ft (1m) tail is the accepted length; this can be lengthened or shortened depending on the way the fish are feeding.

The approach to the water

Unlike float fishing, which often involves a lot of movement, casting, mending line and loose feeding, legering tends to be a relaxed method of fishing. However, it is important that you position yourself and your tackle properly. On stillwaters always try to position your rod at a 45° angle to the bank, with the rod tip no more than 12in (30cm) from the water.

A mistake made by many anglers is that they set up their tackle and then proceed to catapult five or six balls of groundbait into their chosen swim, only to find after their first cast that they have put their bait into the middle of a weed bed, which is impossible to fish.

Before you start fishing you need to establish two things: firstly, whether there are any snags in your chosen swim; and secondly, how deep the water is. Both of these questions can be answered quite simply. Having tied your bomb direct to your 3 or 4lb (1.35 or 1.80kg) reel line, and before tying on your hook length, cast out to your chosen area; as the bomb hits the water, close your bail arm and watch your tip, counting slowly at the same time. When the bomb reaches the bottom of the lake, the tip – be it a swing, quiver or springtip – will drop back. As a rule of thumb, a ⅜oz (10g) bomb will normally fall at a rate of 2ft (60cm) per second, so if you have a count of five your chosen swim is approximately 10ft (3m) deep. Having satisfied yourself that the depth of water is to your liking, with your rod tip pointing down towards the water, slowly wind your bomb back towards you, this will tell you the condition of the lake bed between you and your swim. If there is a snag you may possibly lose your bomb, but better that, than waste 4–5lb (1.80–2.20kg) of expensive groundbait.

Because there is no visible indicator to tell you exactly where the hookbait is lying on the lake bed, feeding when legering is rather more difficult than when float fishing. Again this is an area where anglers – through lack of thought – handicap themselves. Before your first cast, always find a marker to aim at, a tree or bush on the far bank, a buoy in the water. It is impossible to cast a bomb into a 30-acre lake without a marker and then expect to be able to feed accurately; not even the best anglers in the country can do that. Always cast to a marker.

Another problem which often confronts the less experienced angler is that of tightening up to his bomb. This is caused by allowing line to spill off the spool until the bomb hits the lake bed, causing a large bow to develop in the line between the angler and his bomb. Until the line is tightened, the angler is not fishing efficiently. An easy way to overcome this problem is to over-cast your baited area by the depth you are fishing; i.e., if the lake is 10ft (3m) deep, you over-cast by that amount. As your bomb hits the water, close the bail arm on your reel. This will cause two things to happen: firstly, because your line is now tight to the bomb, the bomb will fall back on to your baited area; secondly, as the bomb reaches the lake bed, your tip will drop back. Two turns of the reel will take up what little slack line there is and almost immediately you are fishing efficiently.

Legering in running water

The ability to fish a stationary bait can be just as effective in fast moving rivers like the Trent, the Derwent and the Severn as it can be on still or slow-moving waters. The fundamental difference in approach concerns the position of the rod in the rest. Obviously the key, to success in leger fishing in running water is the ability to keep the bomb still in the area where the fish are feeding. It is a simple matter to cast in and allow the bomb to swing round until it takes up a stationary position, but unfortunately that is seldom where the fish are. In moving water, never be afraid to use extra lead. Using a paternoster rig, the fish must move your tip before it feels the lead, so the size of the bomb used in no way detracts from your ability to get bites. The important point is to keep the bait still. Another cause of bombs moving in moving water is water pressure on the line. For this reason, it is advisable to position your rod upwards on this type of water, so that you minimize the actual amount of line in the water.

For this type of venue, the quivertip is a must; there are various types on the market, but like floats many are designed to catch anglers rather than fish. The most popular quivertips are the tapered ones approximately 10 in (25 cm) in length. It pays to carry a number in differing strengths so that any eventuality can be coped with; obviously a tip which is ideal for a low sluggish river in the summer is not going to prove quite as effective when the river is carrying 3 ft (1 m) of flood water in February; so be prepared for all conditions.

A selection of swimfeeders.

The swimfeeder

First developed many years ago, the swimfeeder – or feeder as it is commonly known – didn't really become an integral part of the angler's tackle until the mid-1970s, when massive bags of barbel began to fall to the feeder/maggot combination on the River Severn.

What makes the feeder so devastating? The feeder is, in effect, a mechanical feeder. Provided that an angler can cast reasonably accurately, he can catch fish using the feeder because, as he has to physically fill the feeder before each cast, he ensures that a steady flow of bait is being deposited into his swim. If he casts every ten minutes or so, the swim will be kept alive. It is understandable that some anglers would like to see the feeder banned, as it can create 'instant' anglers. This might not be a good thing for match angling, but anything that helps anglers catch more fish must be a good thing for the sport.

Types of feeder

In recent years many different feeders have appeared on the market, most of which do the job quite effectively. There are two types of feeder: the open-ended type, which is used in conjunction with groundbait; and the blockend type, which is designed to carry maggots.

Let us look first at the open-ended feeder. This can either be open at both ends or, as is the modern trend, open only at the bottom. This type of feeder is popular on still or slow waters where bream or tench are the quarry. The normal practice is to fill the feeder with hook samples, then plug the end with groundbait. After casting, allow a couple of minutes for the groundbait plug to soak, then give your reel a half turn, this will deposit your hookbait very close to the contents of your feeder, which will have spilled out. The beauty of the open-ended feeder is that a greater variety of baits can be used: because of the large open end, sweetcorn or even luncheon meat can be put into it.

However, on faster-moving rivers like the Severn, where very often the killing bait is maggot, or on waters where the introduction of groundbait has an adverse effect on the fishing, the blockend feeder comes into its own. It is filled with maggots or pinkies, which crawl out on the river bed. The feeder is simplicity itself, yet it has accounted for many, many fish.

The top specimen hunters have modified the feeders so that they are more aero-dynamic and are now fishing at distances of up to 88 yd (80 m) on the large reservoirs. The match anglers are no longer fishing 8 lb (3.50 kg) line tied direct to size 10 hooks; now it is 3 lb (1.35 kg) line, 1.7 lb (0.77 kg) hook length and size 18 or 20 hooks.

Method of fishing

Anglers are great innovators. A new method like the feeder begins to make an impact, and before very long the specimen hunters are modifying it to suit their purposes, whilst at the other end of the chain the match anglers are doing likewise. But unlike other methods, the feeder can be very effective even in its simplest form.

On stillwaters a straightforward 9 ft (2.75 m) leger rod/quivertip combination is adequate, with 3 or 4 lb (1.35 or 1.80 kg) line, depending on the size of feeder used or the distance cast. Using the paternoster rig as described in the section on legering, there is no reason why fish should not be caught provided that the angler can cast reasonably accurately.

Because it is impossible to cast into exactly the same spot every time, little clumps of maggots or casters tend to be deposited around the swim, which does not induce a shoal of fish to stop. The result is that you only catch one or two fish as the shoal passes by. However, if the feeder is dropped on to a bed of groundbait, the area will become much more appetising to the fish.

The feeder has proved that it can be equally, if not even more, devastating on moving water, especially when chub and barbel are present. The secret here is to keep the feeder still. Many anglers do not realize that allowing the feeder to move succeeds only in baiting up an area of river that is much too large to concentrate the fish. Furthermore, by allowing the feeder to swing round in the current, when it does eventually stop moving it will invariably be empty, having left the contents elsewhere. Always make sure that there is enough lead on the feeder to keep it stationary in the current.

Most of the feeders currently available are adequate for most circumstances, but there is not one single feeder that will cope with all the different situations that confront the angler, so you should carry a selection. Do not be afraid to experiment; both specimen hunters and match anglers have and in doing so they have increased their catches.

Pole fishing

Not many seasons ago, the angler seen using a pole was often the target for jokes and laughter. Now, however, the smiles have faded and the jokes come less often, because during the past few years there has been something of a pole revolution in this country, particularly among the match angling fraternity.

It is inevitable that the pole will eventually find its way into every match angler's holdall, and that many pleasure anglers will come to appreciate its use; inevitable, because it is a fact that in the right conditions the pole is unbeatable.

When it comes to catching small fish at close range, the pole is often far superior to our tradi-

The feeder on a sliding link.

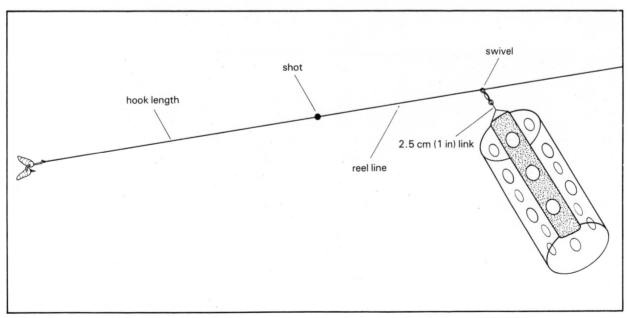

Fishing the Grand Union Canal for roach and skimmer bream at Muscott Mill near Daventry.

tional rod and line. With the addition of the elastic shock absorber it becomes an even more versatile weapon. Fish up to 2 lb (900 g) can also be dealt with successfully. It is only when the need arises to fish further out from the bank than, say, 30 ft (9 m) or to long trot, that our normal running line tackle comes into its own. The angler who is conversant with both the pole and traditional running line tackle is the best equipped of all.

There are two types of pole, the softer telescopic and the more rigid take-apart.

The telescopic pole

The less commonly used is the telescopic pole. It has a soft action all through, and the line is tied direct to the tip. This type of pole is ideal when small fish are encountered in quantity, particularly on the surface or in shallow water, and it is ideal for fishing at speed. The ideal material, naturally enough, is fibreglass. The reason a soft action is required is that when fishing at speed, especially for bleak, there is less effort required in casting with this type of pole. Also, and again especially with bleak, the soft action prevents the fish being pulled off the hook when you strike.

The take-apart pole

The more common and versatile pole is the take-apart type, built to hold a metal crook and elastic shock absorber or a flick tip, depending on the type of fishing you are doing.

What should you look for when buying this type of pole? There are two main points: rigidity and lightness. Fibreglass is the ideal material for the latter consideration. The best poles combine these two qualities to produce the right medium, unlike the traditional fishing rod, which has to be soft actioned for both casting and striking, the pole can be made rigid and more manageable, as the tackle is simply swung out, the elastic cushioning the strike.

On the continent, an angler will have a range of three or more poles, varying in length between 6½–30 ft (2–10 m); even in this country a range of poles is required on many waters. The beginner should start with a single pole of 20 ft (6 m) in length. Many anglers seem to forget that because the pole can be fished in sections, it makes sense to purchase the longest pole you can afford. It is easy to fish with 10 ft (3 m) of a 20 ft (6 m) pole but impossible to fish 20 ft (6 m) if your pole is only 10 ft (3 m) long.

The biggest mistake many newcomers to pole

fishing make is that they often have far too much line between the pole tip and float, thus defeating the pole's great advantage: superior control over tackle. When using the type of rigid pole just described, the nearer your float is to the tip of the pole, the better. Ideally, the float should be no more than 3 ft (1 m) from the pole tip, so that whatever the conditions you have maximum control over your tackle. This ability to control your tackle so perfectly, and thus present your bait in the most natural manner, is the superior advantage given by the pole.

The flick tip

This looks rather like a long quiver tip; it has the line tied directly to it and is used for small fish. This is the ideal sort of pole to use when bloodworm fishing, unless you expect to catch fish over, say, 4 oz (115 g).

The crook

The alloy crook and elastic shock absorber need to be explained in more depth because, correctly used, these items of tackle absolutely paralyze fish and give you an advantage that no item of British tackle can.

The alloy crook is fitted to the top of your pole where it 'crooks' downwards between the pole and the terminal tackle. It is designed to hold the elastic shock absorber and is either a part of the pole when you buy it, or can be purchased separately afterwards.

The purpose of the crook is twofold. Firstly, it minimizes the possibility of tangles; and secondly, it enables you to change your tackle at will. The elastic is fitted at the end of your crook. It is attached by slotting a loop of elastic into the slit at the end of the crook, and it is held in place by sliding a fitted piece of plastic tubing down over the loop.

The elastic comes in four strengths, and will stretch to five or six times its own length. Over the counter, it is sold in pre-wound lengths and is cut to the required length by the angler at home.

The main advantage of the elastic is that it

The metal crook and elastic shock absorber fitted to the top of a pole.

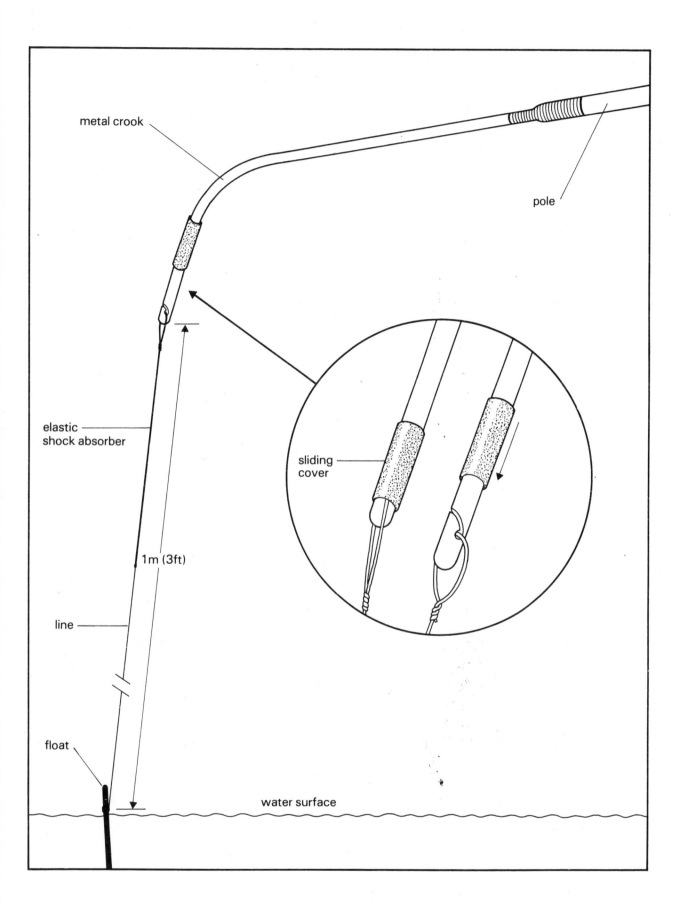

metal crook

pole

elastic
shock absorber

1m (3ft)

line

sliding
cover

float

water surface

enables you to use delicate terminal tackle. A continental angler will often be using the elastic in conjunction with line of 8oz (0.25kg) breaking strain; the hook itself may be as small as 26. The elastic absorbs any initial pull, whenever a decent-sized fish is hooked and therefore protects the fragile tackle.

Yet another advantage of the elastic is evident when a fish pulls the elastic under tension. The further the fish travels from the pole, the stronger the tension becomes. Eventually the fish follows the line of least resistance, giving in to the tension applied by the elastic. If large fish are to be landed with the pole and light tackle, the elastic shock absorber is a necessity.

Terminal rigs

The exact pole rig to use with your alloy crook and flick tip obviously depends on conditions on the day, the venue and so on. However, these rigs are generally made up at home by the individual angler and kept on plastic pole winders, always ready to be looped on to the crook or flick tip when conditions demand. In fact, many continental anglers carry as many as 300 such winders around with them. One of the main reasons for this is that it is difficult to make up such tackle on the bank. Because of the delicate nature of the floats one is able to use when pole fishing, they require very careful shotting, often with tiny shot – a task that is difficult enough on the kitchen table at home!

Chapter 4
Pike fishing

Of all the fish in our lakes and rivers, pike are without doubt the most abused. Many anglers believe, quite wrongly, that pike destroy fisheries. In fact, with few exceptions, the opposite is true. Pike, like all predators, retain a balance within their environment. Lions do not endeavour to eat every zebra, nor do they waste their energy trying to catch the fittest animal in the herd, they feed on the old and infirm animals and then only when they are hungry. Exactly the same situation exists with pike. More important is the fact that fish, unlike animals, cannot leave behind a diseased member of the shoal, particularly in stillwaters, and this is where pike play a major part in keeping disease among fish to a minimum. Without these predators, it is possible for a whole fishery to be wiped out by a single disease.

Many anglers assume that pike swim around with their mouths open, mopping up roach and bream rather like a vacuum cleaner. In fact, pike feed for short periods only each day, maybe for only one hour, and having fed, they are satisfied. That pike will take a dead bait is evidence that they eat dead fish. It is not unreasonable to assume that in a mixed fishery holding as many as 100,000 fish, there are a number of fish dying of natural causes at any one time, and these fish obviously contribute greatly to a pike's staple diet. Why anglers should assume that fish never die of old age is totally beyond my comprehension. The fact is, that anglers choose to believe the worst of pike.

Tackle

Many pleasure anglers will, during the course of a session, set up a rod using a shop-bought Fishing Gazette type pike float, fix a couple of trebles into a live bait and cast it out, leaving it to fish for itself. They then carry on fishing for roach or whatever, and sometime later they notice that the pike float has either disappeared or is being towed across the surface. Invariably by this time the damage is done. The hooks are deep into the pike's throat and unless the angler knows exactly how to deal with this situation, and owns a good pair of artery forceps, the fish is as good as dead.

However, this situation need not exist. If you are going to take up pike fishing, make sure you are properly equipped. A good pike rod is essential; a discarded 6 ft (1.85 m) boat rod is not the answer. As with match rods, the advent of fibreglass has meant that there is now a good selection of pike rods on the market. You do not need an enormous bung to hold up a 2 oz (55 g) roach, and the same applies to trebles. Time and time again you see anglers using barbed trebles, which are much too large for the baits they are using. Many of today's top pike anglers are using size 12 and 14 trebles with only the hook which is inserted into the bait barbed. The barbs on the other two hooks are either snipped off or flattened. This obviously makes unhooking the fish that much easier. Shop-bought trebles and traces are all right, but invariably the hooks are too big and too close together, and the traces are too thick. As with all fishing, the thinking angler catches the most fish. There is no point in using size 6 trebles and 30 lb (14 kg) wire traces if a size 12 treble and 18 lb (8.10 kg) wires traces will do the job better.

The problem is that the angler who buys his trebles and traces from the local tackle shop is invariably inexperienced. He ties his line direct to the wire trace. When he gets a run and it is put under pressure the wire trace often cuts through the monofilament line, causing a breakage. The pike escapes and is left to gorge the bait, complete with trebles. This could be overcome quite simply by using a swivel to join the wire and the nylon. If anglers could be persuaded to make up their own traces they would in fact be fishing with a better product. Treble hooks can be bought in a selection of sizes from most good tackle shops, and Sea Strand trolling wire and Marlin steel wire are available from most specialist shops. These are both excellent multi-strand wires. There was a

Pete Evans lands a Loch Lomond pike.

Barry Burton plays a large Fenland pike.

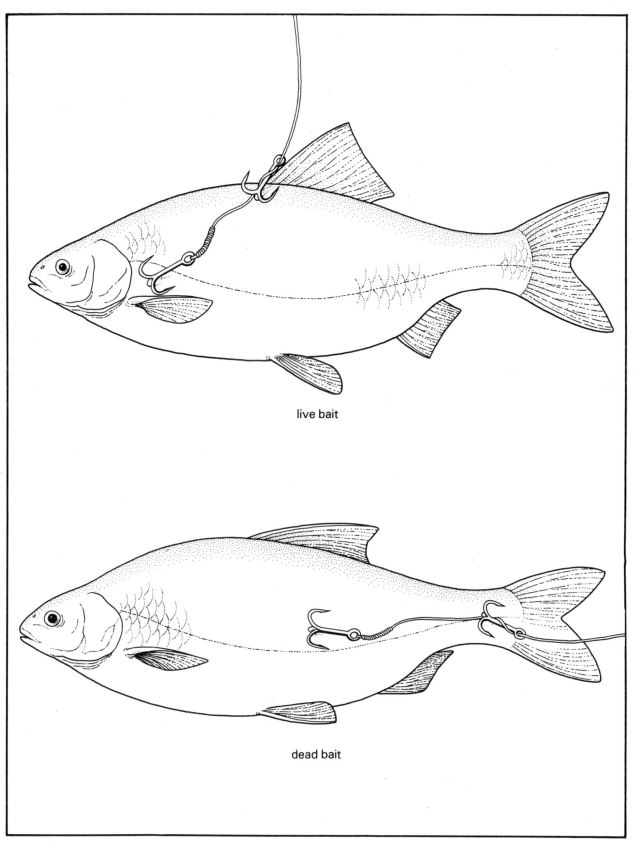

live bait

dead bait

The correct method of baiting the hooks.

move some time ago to single strand wire, but unfortunately this type of wire kinks and when it does so, it can be broken like cotton.

Baiting the hook

When it comes to mounting a bait, the secret is to mount it in such a position that however the pike takes it, either one or both trebles will be in its mouth. Always remember that a deep-hooked pike is a dead pike, so we want to be sure that the hooks are in the mouth, not the throat. Most people will have read or been told that when a run occurs, they should count to ten and then strike. I have even read a book in which the writer has described smoking a cigarette whilst the pike towed his bait around. This is all nonsense. When your float goes under or starts to move, then your bait and hook, if it is mounted properly, are in the pike's mouth so strike immediately. You might lose the odd fish, but you are not going to kill any. *Always strike immediately a run occurs.*

When you are using a small live bait, that is a 1–2 oz (30–55 g) fish, it is not necessary to use two trebles; one semi-barbless treble set into the dorsal fin will do the job. Any pike, even one of 3 lb (1.30 kg), will take a bait of this size straight into its mouth. When using a larger bait, place a treble under the dorsal fin to take the impact of the cast, and the second in the muscle surrounding the pectoral fin. Do not place the trebles too far apart. When fishing with dead baits, one treble will generally be inserted in the tail root so it is asking for trouble to place the second in the head or the gill cover, the pike takes the bait head first and the hooks must go down its throat. Always try to keep the hooks as far back as possible.

There has been some conjecture in recent years that if a deeply-hooked pike is returned to the water with the hooks still in its throat, its natural juices will in some way dissolve the hook. However, there is little evidence to support this view. If you catch a pike and you cannot get the hooks out, kill it quickly and painlessly. Of course, the answer is to avoid deep-hooking them in the first place.

Young anglers often fish for pike and then, having caught one, are terrified to go near it. This is foolishness. Once a pike is on the bank he is in no mood for a fight; he is dying. Ask yourself, if you were drowning, would you be looking to stay in the water? Of course not. All the pike wants to do is get back into the water, so get those hooks out and put him back. Never use a gaff; fortunately, this practice is not seen much these days.

Pike fishing can be exciting but always try to remember that future generations will only be able to enjoy good fishing if we conserve our fisheries.

Live baits or dead baits?

Anglers often ask whether it is morally right to fish with live baits, when dead baits are so effective, as are plugs and spinners. The answer is, that it is a matter for each man's conscience. Live baits do account for many fish.

Dr Barrie Rickards and Ray Webb, in their book on pike fishing, stated that at certain times, dead baits were the most effective bait, whilst on other occasions they were unable to get a bite on a dead bait and yet in the same swim a live bait would be snapped up immediately. Much in the same way as on occasions bream will not take a float-fished maggot, but will take the bait if it is legered.

Part 2 Flyfishing

Chapter 5
Tackle for trout fishing

Still waters in which trout are found vary enormously. At the top end of the scale are the vast Scottish lochs and Irish loughs, the big natural lakes of the English Lake District, and reservoirs, waters like these are fished from the bank and by boat, with widely varying techniques being used.

At the lower end of the scale are the little pools, maybe only an acre or two, which are run as put-and-take fisheries, and there is a big middle ground comprising both mountain and lowland natural lakes and dams, varying from around fifteen acres up to perhaps a hundred acres or so.

The trout in these waters are as varied in size as the waters are, and to make the most of both the environment and the fish it is necessary to use a wide range of lines and rods.

Rods for stillwater fishing

The popular conception of a stillwater trout rod is of one at least 9 ft (2.75 m) and up to 10½ ft (3.20 m), stiff enough to cast a size 8 or 9 line. Such combinations hopelessly overgun most trout (and trout fishermen), so that the person is exhausted in an hour or so and any fish he catches can show comparatively little fight.

The important point about any flyrod is that it should suit the user's physique, ability and his personal whim.

If you can afford them graphite (carbon fibre) rods are by far the best. The reasons for this are that they are lighter than hollow glass-fibre or split bamboo cane, and therefore less tiring to use. They are thinner, and therefore have less wind resistance when casting and when fishing in a gale. The material recovers from bending more quickly than glass or cane, and having done so it does not continue to wobble, so, since the flyline in the air follows every movement of the rod tip, the graphite rod casts a straighter line than either of the other two materials.

Hollow-glass rods are much cheaper than graphite and the better ones fish very well indeed. Until recently the main problem with the material was that, to get the crisp but smooth action, it was necessary to have a very thick tubular section near the handle – very ugly and presenting great wind resistance. Modern constructions in glass have avoided much of that problem.

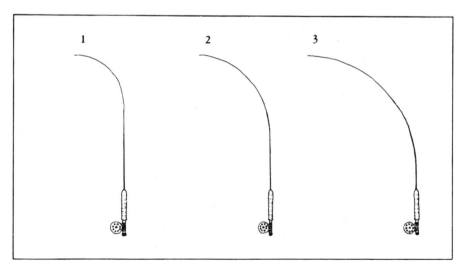

Types of flyrod action
1 Tip (fast) action.
2 Middle-to-tip (medium) action.
3 Through (butt) action.

Cane rods are beautiful – or the best ones are – but in lengths above about 8 ft (2.45 m) they can be too heavy for constant stillwater use.

For flyfishing from a boat on lakes and reservoirs, a 10 ft (3.05 m) graphite rod with a fairly easy action, matched to a DT 5 or 6 line is suitable.

While it is the blank, or shaft, of the rod that is its most important part, whatever it is made from, the quality of the rings, cork handle and reel-holder must be good, otherwise the rod will soon fail. For example, a set of poor quality rings can be grooved in two days of fishing by the abrasion of the line.

Tip and butt rings must be of very hard material, since they have to take abrasion from the line at various angles. Only rings with a hard-chromed surface, or of tungsten-carbide, or lined with aluminium oxide are suitable. For the intermediate rings, the snake ring, with a hard-chrome finish, is lighter than the other designs, such as the single-leg Fuji rings that are lined with aluminium oxide, and may be whipped to the rod much more firmly.

Cork handles should be hard and fairly slim, although the thickness of the handle should match the size of the fisherman's hands. Thick ones may be sanded down to suit. I have never felt the need for screw-type reel seats on flyrods, and favour a fixed clip at the extremity of the handle with a sliding ring to hold the reel's front foot. The parallel part of the handle to which the reel is fitted may simply be the cork, suitably reduced in diameter, or a section of hardwood, drilled and glued on to the rod butt, on which the clip and ring are fitted.

The joints of hollow-glass and graphite rods are usually of the spigot type, in which a reduced thick-walled tube of the rod material – or even a solid piece – is glued into the upper end of the butt section to fit into the open end of the tip section. There are variations on this, in which there is an enlarged section on the tip section to accept the butt, or a similar thicker piece on the lower section into which the tip fits. Spigot or similar joints should not fit together so well that the two halves of the blank touch when the rod is assembled; a gap of about ¼ in (6 mm) allows for take-up over the years when wear reduces the comparatively

soft, mated materials. This abrasion-induced wear may be retarded by rubbing the male part of the joint with a candle, thus coating it and preventing contact between the soft materials. But the wax should be removed periodically, with white spirit, and then renewed, to avoid the build-up of abrasive grit.

Cane rods are usually joined by metal ferrules, of brass, chemically turned a bronze or blue colour, or of nickel silver, similarly coloured, although some are left silver. The latter ferrules are best and more expensive. Again, they should not mate fully, but a gap of about ⅛ in (3 mm) should show on the connected sections of a new rod, to allow for wear. They should be kept clean and very lightly wiped with olive oil – not a mineral oil – before assembly.

Lines for stillwater fishing

In general terms, choose the lightest line that will do the job. A light line may be cast on the water gently; it sets up less resistance, from friction across and through the water, such as when a trout takes the fly and when it is being played, than a thicker, heavier line; and a light line on a light, slim flexible rod increases the enjoyment of playing the fish. The lightest flyrod obtainable is quite capable, in skilled hands, of bringing to net a trout of 10 lb (4.5 kg); and light rods are less tiring.

However, light flylines and toothpick rods have their limitations. One cannot expect to cast a big, heavy fly or lure vast distances on a light line; the line just has not got the weight to carry the big, air-resistant fly. Nor will a very light line cast easily into a strong wind; and if much sunk-line fishing is to be done, specially from a boat over deep water, a heavy, fast-sinking line will be needed, for a light sinking line will waste good fishing time – one has to wait too long before it sinks to a fishing depth. There need be only one criterion: will the chosen line cast the size of flies you need to use, on the water you plan to fish, and do so on a rod that is capable of being used by you for a long day?

For stillwater trout fishing, line weights between size 3 and size 8 will cope with most situations. If you plan to do much boat fishing on big, deep reservoirs where large trout lie deep in the water for much of the time – waters like Grafham Water and Rutland, for example – you may need to have a size 9 fast-sinking line and a rod to match.

Crouching to keep a low profile, the fisherman casts to trout feeding beneath the willows along this lovely little Hampshire chalk-stream, the Wallop Brook, a tributary of the famous Test.

DOUBLE TAPER (usually 27.4 m/30 yd)

level tip   level belly   level (spare) tip

WEIGHT-FORWARD TAPER (27.4-32 m/30-35 yd)

level tip   level belly   level dressed shooting line

SHOOTING TAPER (9-13.7 m/10-15 yd)

level tip   level belly   glued splice

thin braided monofilament nylon shooting line

Flyline profiles.

The profile of a line is signified by an internationally accepted key: double-taper is DT; weight-forward is WF; and shooting-taper is ST. Further, a floating line is signified by the letter F, a sinking line by S, and a line that floats, but sinks at the tip (a floating/sinking line) by F/S.

The most widely-used type of line is the double-taper. This is usually 30 yd (9.1 m) long, level in the centre, with 8–12 ft (2.4–3.6 m) tapered at each end. In trout fishing, the double-taper line is mainly used floating, or with the centre part floating and both tips sunk. It may be turned round on the reel when one end becomes cracked and worn, so extending its useful life.

For making consistently long casts, a weight-forward line may be used. This consists of a front section similar to the front of a double-taper line, with the line becoming thinner, down to some thin, level, shooting line. When casting the weight-forward line, only the front section is projected outside the rod tip, and the cast is made to send the heavy front section out at speed, dragging the slim, shooting line, which has less resistance in the rod rings, behind it.

The weight-forward line makes regular casting distances of 25 yd (22.8 m) reasonably easy, but demands casting skill since it is necessary to project the heavy front part of the line at high speed, generally at a higher elevation than a double-taper line needs, to attain the ranges of which it is capable. The weight-forward line will never land as gently as the former, since all its casting weight is concentrated near the end.

Weight-forward lines are made to float throughout their length, or to sink over the final 10 ft (3 m) or so, but with the rest of the line floating, or to sink completely – slowly, quickly, or very quickly.

The type of line that can be cast farthest of all – and that means fastest as well – is the shooting-taper or shooting-head, as it is more commonly known. In essence, the shooting-taper is like the weight-forward line except that, the shooting line behind the heavy front belly is very much thinner than the dressed line on the weight-forward taper, and therefore slips through the rings of the rod, and through the air, much more quickly and easily. The competent performer with a shooting-taper will consistently cast 35 yd (32 m) or more in favourable conditions; and with a following wind and no obstructions behind 50 yd (45.7 m) is possible. However, such lines cannot be made to alight with delicacy on the water regularly. They tend to fold back on themselves, because of the absence of friction, instead of unrolling in a loop as does the double-taper line.

Shooting-tapers are very useful to the lure fisherman, who needs to cast a long way with a minimum of backward and forward rod movements. They are at their best as sinking lines, because once they are on the water as floaters, there is nothing the fisherman can do to control them, except pull them in. However, shooting-tapers of floating line are useful, more particularly to the reservoir bank angler on hard-fished waters where, quite frequently towards the middle and back-end of the season, fish become very wary of coming too close to the margins, having seen too many lines and flies cast by too many fishermen.

The code of figures which describes the various weights of flylines begins at 1 and goes up to 12. For most flyfishing on stillwaters a size 6 or 7 floating double-taper line will do the job. For really delicate presentation and the ability to see takes and lift them like lightning, a floating DT 3 or 4 line is a revelation. And since it is used on a very slim wand of a rod, very fragile leaders may be used, with tiny flies, the flex in the rod and the lack of friction of the thin line in the water permitting big fish to be handled.

Once one gets used to using the light line and matching rod, one can learn little tricks that will beat wind and other problems. Remember, always, that is is the speed of the line that counts when after distance. A light line at high speed may be cast 30 yd (27 m), the flyline-backing splice going up the rod rings, in good conditions. A light line, however, loses velocity more quickly than a heavy line because it lacks the mass to carry.

Flylines vary widely in quality. Some companies make good floating lines, but bad sinkers, and vice versa. Sink-tip lines (F/S) are notoriously difficult to cast well, due to the sudden change in density of the two materials necessary to float the back end and sink the tip. Flylines are made in many colours, and highly-visible floating lines will show by their movement when a fish takes the sunken fly. However, some fishermen believe that fish can see such bright lines. Sinking lines should be dark grey, green or brown.

Flylines are expensive, and they should be carefully maintained to last and perform well. All modern vinyl-coated lines must be kept clean, by wiping down after every trip with a soft cloth or paper tissue damped with fresh water. Some manufacturers provide a tin of cleaner and conditioner. Line coatings are damaged by cracking, mainly because they are whip-lashed when casting, although treading on them in boats, on hard banks, or using them coated with particles of grit will also cause damage. Oil-derived chemicals also damage lines. Prolonged exposure to strong sunlight should be avoided: for example, do not leave the reel in the back window of a car for weeks on end.

Rods and lines for river fishing

Use a delicate rod whenever possible, a floating double-taper line as light as will do the job, and leaders of 8–12 ft (2.4–3.6 m) long tapered to sizes suitable for use with flies that can range from size 18 up to size 10. A tippet of just over 1 lb (450 g) test may sometimes catch a fish when no heavier one will.

Reels

Reels for stillwater flyfishing should be as light as possible and between 3¼–3½ in (80–90 mm) in diameter. Single action or multiplying reels are suitable; automatic recovery reels are not – the only model with sufficient line and backing capacity is too heavy at 9 oz (255 g), the rest are too small.

Reels with perforated drums are best. They are lighter, since there is less metal in them, and the holes allow water to drain from the line and its backing after use. Many flyfishers hold the view that the reel is unimportant: that provided it holds the line, it will do.

It must have a very smooth-running check or ratchet mechanism, preferably with an adjustable spring to apply more or less pressure to the running fish as it drags line from the reel. Any jerky motion from a reel with a roughly cut or large-toothed ratchet wheel can cause breakage of slim nylon leaders, or tear out the little hook, or break or distort the fine steel wire of the hook. All these have drums with exposed rims, on which manual pressure may be applied against a running fish approaching trouble, such as a sunken snag or weed-beds. Other reels also have excellent check mechanisms but have the rim of the drum running inside the frame of the reel, and manual pressure may then only be applied by putting a finger between the sideplates of the drum and on to the line itself. This is somewhat tricky and less delicate than a smooth rim of metal.

A much cheaper reel with an exposed drum rim is the English Intrepid 'Rimfly'. It is not made to the fine tolerances or finish of the Hardy and Orvis reels, and has a rather coarse ratchet mechanism, but it does sterling service, a little molybdenum disulphide grease, such as MTS 1000 by Rocol, will smooth it out quite considerably. It is perfectly adequate for use with leaders of 5–6 lb (2.2–2.7 kg) test.

Each rod you own needs a reel to go with it containing a matching line; if lines that float, sink or have sinking tips are to be used on the same rod, spare spools for the reel containing those lines can save extra expense in buying more than one reel. In practice, however, a lightweight rod with size 3 or 4 line will seldom be used for anything but a floating line; sink-tip lines of those sizes are seldom available, sizes 5–6 being the lightest. A rod for a size 6 line might well have a reel with spare spools for floating, sinking and sink-tip lines, however.

Leaders

The leader has to do many things: first and foremost it forms a comparatively invisible link between the thick flyline and the fly; it places the fly, and itself, gently on the water; and its length may be used, varied by the use of grease (to make the nylon float) or some form of detergent (to make it sink) to fish the fly slowly at any depth between ½in (12mm) sub-surface to maybe 20ft (6m) down.

The taper can be formed by knotting several different diameters of nylon together, but the disadvantage of so doing is that the knots can impede the sinking rate of the leader and can also create a fish-disturbing wake near the fly in calm water. Also, knots are weak spots, no matter how well tied they are, and the fewer knots in the tackle, the better. Any knotless-tapered leader may be lengthened by joining additional lengths of nylon to it; either a thicker piece than the heavy butt end, or a tippet of the same diameter as the tip, or slightly thinner.

Accessories

Stillwater flyfishing demands a number of accessories. A reliable landing net is essential and the best for bank fishing is a lightweight but strong alloy net with a round or pear-shaped frame that swivels down to lie alongside the handle. It should be of the extending type and have a strong clip to attach to a round brass or stainless steel ring sewn to a ½in (12mm) leather strap worn over the shoulder. The net then hangs down at one's lower back, out of the way, but can be quickly pulled round by the strap and unclipped to land a fish. This is much better than having the net clipped to a ring on a fishing waistcoat under one's free arm – not the rod arm, where it does get in the way. Also, when fishing in wet weather, it is a simple matter to put on a waterproof jacket and sling the net over the top of it, instead of having it beneath the coat on the waistcoat ring, and inaccessible.

For boat fishing, a rigid round frame on a strong handle at least 6ft (1.8m) long is best. Net frames for bank and boat fishing need be no more than 22in (55cm) across, provided the bag-shaped net is at least 2ft (60cm) deep.

Mobility is essential in bank fishing. Some fishermen say they see no use for a net and drag their fish on to the bank, but that cannot be done when using delicate leaders, nor can it be done when wading among marginal weeds that may stretch 20ft (6m) or more out into the water.

Again for reasons of mobility and comfort on the bank, a fishing waistcoat, rather than a haversack, is a necessity, in which to carry gear and food, etc. The multi-pocketed waistcoat distributes the weight of all the gear it holds evenly from both shoulders, with a place for everything and everything in its place.

For boat fishing, which needs better weather protection, and where mobility is not required, a large haversack will carry all the gear required, plus a waterproof hooded parka and overtrousers, since thigh-boots are unnecessary in a boat, wellington boots or similar being adequate.

Boat fishing

Boat fishing, besides requiring a longer, lissom rod, a long-handled landing net and maybe more lures – on reservoirs at any rate – than the bank fisherman needs, also demands other accessories for maximum enjoyment. A cushion to sit on is very important, and since most boat thwarts are so low that, when sitting and fishing, one's knees are under one's chin, many boat specialists carry a long board which they rest across the gunwales of the boat, so that they can sit comfortably in a high position.

A drogue – which is a kind of sea-anchor that slows the drift of a boat in wind – is also necessary. The best is made of nylon, is light, packs into a tiny roll for carrying, and dries quickly. It is also best to carry one's own anchor – a proper one with flukes and at least 4ft (1.2m) of chain between its ring and the 50yd (45.7m) of nylon rope that is sometimes necessary to hold the boat still over deep water in a wind.

Casting

Casting can be learnt only from another good caster who has the ability to pass on his knowledge, and a beginner would be well advised to spend money on a few lessons with a good professional instructor before ever putting line to water. However, there are a few points worth making here. Technique is what counts, not brute force. Grip the rod handle comfortably, not too tightly, with the thumb on top and facing straight up the rod, or with thumb and forefingers forming a cradle, or, for short-range delicate and accurate casts *with a light outfit*, with the forefinger extended up the handle and directly on top – that is, opposite the direction in which the reel faces. The thumb-up is perhaps best, but if it is not comfortable, try another grip.

The backward and forward normal overhead cast should begin slowly and end faster, with a conscious flick to speed up the rod tip and line. The forward cast should be rather like holding a hammer and knocking a nail in a wooden wall directly in front of your shoulder. Always ensure the reel faces directly to the front, with the wrist straight, the hand held as if you were going to punch somebody; the worst mistake of all is to allow the wrist (in a right-handed caster) to bend with the reel facing away to the right. Try knocking a nail in with the wrist bent thus, and you will see that no power can be applied in that way.

Finally, ensure that the loop of line you cast in the air is formed vertically, so that the line travels and turns over directly over the tip of the rod, which should be almost perpendicular, perhaps with a slight bias to the right on the backward movement, which will prevent the line, and the fly, catching on each other due to following *exactly* the same path in both directions.

The right-handed caster should use his reel with the handle to the left, winding being done with the left hand, which avoids changing hands to play a fish.

Chapter 6
Brown and rainbow trout in stillwaters

No water is ever truly still: the surface of the smallest farm pond is ruffled by the wind, thus creating drift. On large waters, wind has a dramatic effect, not only building up large waves, but also creating quite swift currents in the water for up to a day after the wind has fallen. Temperature, too, has its effects, the cool water descending, because it is heavier, to be replaced by warmer water on the surface. Wind cools surface water and also blows it towards the lee shore. It sinks as it travels, causing a current down to quite a considerable depth. The water piles up against the lee shore, then runs back at a lower level.

Trout fishing seasons open in spring; in high mountain country, lakes may still be ice-rimmed in late May. Many a 1 April opening day has been graced with snow and sleet; others have seen blazing sunshine and temperatures in the low 70°s F (20°s C).

A relatively mild winter will mean water temperatures in which trout may feed, although little growth may be shown. On many a 1 April, brown trout in fine condition may be caught; on just as many first days, browns will be lean and still showing the ravages of spawning four or five months before.

Rainbows, being a mixed race now in many parts of Britain, may be in full spawning livery in April, the cocks with big hooked jaws and livid flanks, the hens dull and spilling ripe orange eggs. Both are likely to be slimy and soft to the touch. Yet on the same day as fish in this condition are caught, some rainbows in good shape will be taken, fish that may have got rid of eggs the previous autumn, or reabsorbed them – bright silver fish that fight hard and have pink flesh.

Deep nymph fishing in still water.

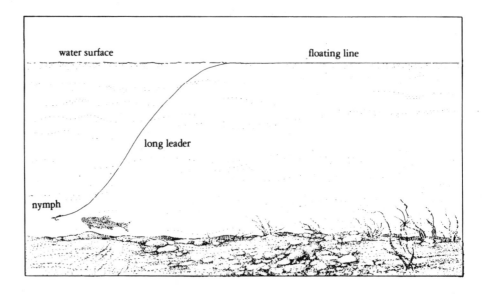

Spring

Since spring days can be rather windy, start by using an 8½ft (2.60m) graphite rod and a double-taper size 6 floating line. Because prevailing winds at this season are often from the south-west, you should choose the north shore, provided the wind is not too strong, since waves create a food larder on the lee shore. Bays and headlands often provide ideal places from which to fish, so that one is casting slightly with and across the wind. It is not the immediate wind that is important, remember, but the one that has prevailed for weeks, or at least days.

In spring, water levels are usually high and the best places to fish are where the water has flooded areas of low bushes, brush, long grasses or hedgerows leading into the water. Insects, shrimps and beetles like to crawl up stems and branches, which also afford them shelter, and trout find their movements above bottom, as well as on it, very attractive.

A 16ft (4.8m) knotless tapered leader should be held with a 5lb (2.2kg) tippet, and 1yd (90cm) of 4lb (1.8kg), if the rules permit. First choice of fly will be a Stickfly, or something similar, on a long-shank size 12 or 10 hook. The hook will have been weighted with lead wire, foil or copper wire before the body dressing was applied, to make the fly sink more quickly and remain at depth when being fished back.

Fish really slowly, keeping an eye rivetted on the tip of the fluorescent line for a sudden jerk, or round-the-bend movement, or a stoppage in the line's drift downwind. In a big ripple, or in difficult light conditions, it may be impossible to see the tip of the line at a range of 20yd (18.3m) or more, in which case there is no alternative but to await a tactile pull – but fish will be lost due to shallow hooking.

The margins may produce a fish, then, or they may not. Once some 20yd (18.3m) or so of line have covered the water, with feet still on dry land, then, and only then, begin to wade slowly and quietly into the water. Fish the spot for half an hour, whether fish have been taken or not, trying the fly just touching bottom up to about mid-water. If the Stickfly does not work, then try a Black and Peacock Spider (leaded) or a size 10 Pheasant Tail Nymph (leaded) with a thorax of natural wild rabbit fur. If these fail too, move to another spot and try all over again.

In very strong wind, it may be necessary to fish with a slow-sinking line that still permits a slow recovery, in which case a weight-forward line will be best. Of course, the takes must then be detected by touch, and again, some fish will undoubtedly be missed, or played briefly before being lost, simply because they detected the fraud, or the hook only obtained a tiny hold in the skin of the jaw and they broke free.

Should the afternoon turn warm, with a few fish taking hatching flies from the surface, it is great fun to fish for them. Fishing for visible trout is far more interesting than searching the depths. If fish are seen to be taking insects at the surface in April, it is most likely they are taking a small Black Midge pupa or an Orange/Silver Midge pupa, both species hatching in that month.

Lure fishing, from the bank or a boat, demands a stiffer rod, heavier line and stronger, shorter leader than is used for fishing imitatively in early season. Successful lures are usually dressed on long-shank hooks, size 8, 6 or even 4, and flies of this size and bulk demand a heavy line to push and pull them through the air. A weight-forward or shooting-taper, size 8, will cast such lures 30–40yd (27.5–36.5m) or more respectively, and fish them deeply if the line is a fast-sinking type.

A size 8 long-shank lure usually needs a 6lb (2.7kg) tippet, to have the stiffness to turn the fly over in the air and to absorb the sudden shock of a fish grabbing the fly while the line is being stripped back in. That is not to say that the line is being, or needs to be stripped back very fast, as many lure fishers may be seen to do. However, even a long, slow pull in one direction, coinciding with a sudden pull in the opposite direction can impose great strain on the leader. Many lure fishers use 10lb (4.5kg) tippets when fishing lures 3in (7.5cm) long or more for big trout.

Early season trout appear to take black lures best – patterns like Black Lure, Black Marabou, Sweeney Todd. The black will also catch fish in summer, but often white does well on an evening when darkness comes sooner than it should. In bright summer weather, an orange fly can be deadly. White Marabou or Bob Church's Appetiser are both good; the orange range is well represented by such patterns as Whisky and Price's Orange Streamer.

A rod of 9–9½ft (2.75–2.90m) for the size 8 line will carry the big, air-resistant fly well clear of one's head on the forward cast, and has the stiffness to punch it out a long way, even into a wind. When lure fishing at depths of 15ft (4.5m) or

Left column, top to bottom: *Damselfly Nymph number 1, Damselfly Nymph number 2, Sedge Pupa number 3, Sedge Pupa number 1, Sedge Pupa number 2;* middle column, top to bottom: *Sedge Larva number 1, Sedge Larva number 3, Sedge Larva number 2, Pond Olive Nymph, Pheasant Tail Nymph, Claret Nymph, Shrimp;* right column top to bottom: *Black Midge Pupa, Red Midge Pupa, Pale Green Midge Pupa, Olive Midge Pupa, Golden Dun Midge Pupa, Orange/Silver Midge Pupa, Phantom Midge Pupa, Fluorescent Red Midge Pupa, Fluorescent Green Midge Pupa.*

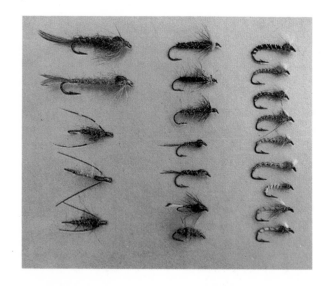

Top left, *Vulture (Matuka style),* middle left, *Esox-it (pike fly),* bottom left, *estuary seatrout lure;* top right, *Black Marabou,* middle right, *White Marabou,* bottom right, *estuary seatrout lure.*

more, a long cast – at least 25yd (23m), and better, 40yd (37m) – is necessary so that the fly fishes at depth for as long a distance as possible before the angle of the line to the rod tip begins to pull it to the surface again.

Since long casting with heavy weight-forward lines and shooting-tapers causes considerable surface disturbance, it is best, in general, to select deep water close to the bank, and water with wind on it to produce a ripple. Ripple camouflages disturbance from the fish.

Early-season boat fishing on reservoirs and lakes, which includes the big natural Scottish and Irish ones, is usually done with sinking lines, too. The boat is either anchored over suitable water and the anglers fish downwind or down and across, or it is allowed to drift as slowly as possible with the wind, its progress slowed by a drogue, which is an underwater parachute on a cord. Some reservoir fishermen use a collapsible rudder, which is fixed to the transom and used to steer the drifting boat at a fixed distance from the bank, following its outline into bays and round headlands.

On the big natural lakes, teams of traditional wet flies, winged and hackled patterns, are popular, and they are usually fished 2–3ft (80–90cm) down, on the drift, no matter what the water depth. Brown trout in natural lakes are more likely to be feeding in cold surface water than stocked rainbows, and the method can be quite effective.

On reservoirs, however, the use of sinking shooting-tapers joins that of traditional flyfishing on the drift, and the big lures are fished as described from the bank. Wherever possible, though, experienced reservoir boat fishers will anchor over deep water, close to the dam face or where there are drop-offs or trenches in the lake bed, to get their lines and lures down deep and fish them back slowly. In cold water trout are not inclined to chase after their food as they are in the warmer temperatures of late spring and summer.

In a mild spring, mid-May sees the beginning of the best trout flyfishing on still waters. Several species of midges will by then be hatching, plus upwing flies like Lake and Pond Olives, the Sepia Dun, which may hatch in a warm April, some land-bred flies that get blown on to the water, and there will be increased activity of many other forms of water life.

With water temperatures at about 52°F (11°C) minimum up to about 60°F (15°C) during this transitional period (the measurement being taken at about 2ft/60cm), both brown and rainbow trout are likely to have discovered that there is an increased amount of insect and other animal food in the upper levels of the water and they are likely to take a fly fished within 1yd (90cm) of the surface, or within ½in (12mm) of the surface, as the case may be. As always, experimentation in fishing depth and speed is the key to success.

From this point in the season onwards, try to remember that trout will want to be feeding as much as they are able. They are voracious, if sometimes delicate feeders, and unless the water is very cold indeed, below 48°F (9°C) or above about 70°F (21°C) the fish will always be where the food is.

With the warmer conditions and more food available, more trout will now be inclined to swim into the marginal shallows, maybe into water 3ft (90cm) deep. Later in the summer, even 1ft (30cm) of water, especially over flooded grass, bushes or weedbeds, is deep enough for fish to venture into.

For bank work, a lightweight graphite rod, between 8–8¾ft (2.45–2.70m) long, is suitable and a size 3–4 double-taper floating line, coloured fluorescent orange for visibility. The knotless-tapered leader, 16–25ft (4.8–7.6m) long, will have a tippet of 3–6lb (1.3–2.7kg) test; if the fishery rules do not permit tippets below 5lb (2.2kg) test, as some state, choose an extra-strong, thin nylon, like Platil Strong, which gives strength with slimness. In 5½lb (2.5kg) test this nylon is thinner than ordinary nylon 1½lb (700g) weaker.

Your choice of fly should be something to imitate a hatching midge pupa of a size and colour likely to be about: a size 12 or 14 black one, or maybe an orange/silver or a pale green. If these fail try a size 12 Pheasant Tail Nymph.

If a fish is seen to rise, cast the fly quickly but gently to the rise, or just on the upwind side if there is a breeze, since fish mainly swim into the wind (surface current). Wait a second or two for the fly to go under, together with several centimetres of the tippet, then move the fly slowly, either by stripping or figure-eight retrieve. If the fish boils near where you think your fly is, quickly lift the rod to tighten the line. If you see the floating part of the leader jerk forward or move in any unusual manner, also tighten. If the line tip does the same, again tighten. Too many fishermen wait until they feel a pull before tightening, and often lose fish or miss them completely.

Mid-May normally sees the beginning of that delightful phenomenon, the evening rise, which may begin as early as 7.30 pm or as late 8.45 pm, which leaves very little time to fish before darkness falls. Again, the midges are nearly always responsible for the rise at this time of the year, since they tend to move towards the surface as the light goes, to hatch. Daytime fishing from this time until well into July will nearly always produce fish, some of which may be seen rising.

It takes confidence to fish a single nymph slowly near the surface where no trout are seen moving, but very often fish will be taken that way. Try to believe that every cast you make, and every retrieve, is going to produce a take.

When fish are feeding within 1 in (2.5 cm) of the surface, even ½ in (12 mm), make sure that you fish your fly no deeper. Use flotant on your leader to within about 1 in (2.5 cm) of the fly to do so. Fish extra slowly, since any drag from where the leader submerges to the fly will cause a minute wake. If your fly is 3 in (7.5 cm) down when fish are swimming subsurface, taking midge pupae hanging from the surface film preparatory to hatching, the trout will never see your fly because the eye of the fish will be, maybe, 1 in (2.5 cm) from the surface and looking up.

When the fly fished down to about 5 ft (1.5 m) produces no takes, and you have tried several different patterns and different speeds and types of recovery, then it may well be that the fish are feeding nearer the bottom, if they are in the area at all. Try the leader nymph for a while, as for the early April style; it often works.

A final word about the evening rise, which applies to such times later in the season too. The rise may often last for only ten or fifteen minutes before the fish stop feeding or go down and out to deeper water. It is essential to be quick to take advantage of this hectic feeding period, since there are days when fishing before and after this brief rise will produce only the odd fish, or none at all. Do not wade in and out of the water to land and kill your fish. Having landed (netted) a trout, kill it quickly with the priest where you stand. Remove the fly, then string the fish on your stringer, attached to your belt, or leave it in the net hanging over your shoulder. Cast again as quickly as possible. This way, you maximize your fishing time and do not cause disturbance by wading to and from the bank. This is why the fishing waistcoat containing all your tackle needs is such an advantage. A bag on the bank is useless.

Droppers are useful for boat fishing during the mid-May onwards period. With one or two droppers and using conventional winged or hackled wet fly patterns – like Butcher, Rogan's Golden Olive, Dunkeld, Black Pennell, Mallard and Claret, for example – the flies are fished on the drift and as they near the boat, the dropper or droppers are lifted to skim along the surface, making a little vee. This is very attractive to trout, especially in a ripple. Most takes will come within 2 ft (60 cm) of the surface and many to the dropper will be visible as the fish splashes at the fly.

Lure fishing from both bank and boat during this period will still catch fish, both deep down and near the surface, but such tactics are not much fun, when fish are feeding properly and willing to take small representations of their natural food.

Summer

Now even more insects will appear. The many types of midge pupae will be joined by the sedges (caddis), which make their presence known in the evenings as they swarm in the margins and over the water, rising and falling in the air and scuttering their ungainly way across the water, like a swan trying to take off. Numerous land-bred and water-bred flies, plus the other food animals like shrimps, various beetles, spiders, water-lice and water-snails, join the increased species of those important midges. By early July damselfly nymphs will be numerous, too.

It is also the time when the dry fly begins to take fish. And this, when the sedges are up in the evenings, can be the cream of the season's sport. As the light fails, trout will begin to rise. The rise will intensify until, on a good, mild and fairly calm evening there are fish everywhere. The air hums with the wing-beats of millions of midges, and sedges flutter like snowflakes. On goes the dry sedge pattern, to match the natural that seems to be most prevalent: it might be a Cinnamon Sedge, or a Welshman's Button, or a Silver Sedge, or Grousewing, or a Red Sedge, or even that mighty beast, the Great Red Sedge, which can be 1 in

The epitome of nymph-fishing concentration: the fisherman tries to keep his leader and line tip in view as the setting sun forms confusing light patterns on the water's surface.

(2.5 cm) long. Or it could be one of many others. The dry fly might need to be on a size 14 hook, to match the size of the smaller sedges, or a size 8 long-shank for the Great Red Sedge. It is first necessary to discover if the frenzied rise of trout is taking midge pupae gathering to hatch beneath the surface, or sedge pupae hatching out, or the hatched winged adult. This is not easy to do, because the fish may begin their feeding on one species of midge and then switch to another that becomes more numerous, or they may switch from the midge to the sedge, or vice versa.

Surface activity does not necessarily indicate feeding on winged sedges. Often, the fish are taking only the sedge pupae as they approach the surface preparatory to hatching and will not accept a hatched, surface-borne fly.

On an evening of calm water conditions, the slightest movement of a midge pupa imitation being fished within 1 in (25 cm), or less, of the surface on a long greased leader, will make a fish-scaring wake, and at such times it is necessary to fish the pupa (or pupae if you use a dropper) absolutely without movement, other than that imported by the surface drift of the water in which the naturals are borne.

Another mid-summer fishing condition that demands a rather special approach is the very hot, bright day with no clouds in the sky and the surface of the water mirror-calm. These conditions make traditional boat-fishing types blanch and seek solace at the nearest pub, or opt for a fast-sinking line and a lure out in the deeps. However, the bank angler – and the boat angler, too, if he can anchor his craft well – can still fish enjoyably and effectively.

In such conditions the fish will be feeding near the bottom at a depth of 12–20 ft (3.6–6 m), avoiding the bright light and, perhaps, the excessively warm top layer of water. The tactic involves finding a steeply sloping area of bank with the requisite depth of water at casting range, then fishing a nymph very slowly close to the bottom.

The double-taper floating line is needed, plus a knotless-tapered leader at least 20 ft (6 m) long, better still 25 ft (7.6 m), and with a tippet of about 5 lb (2.2 kg) test. The nymph itself should be about size 10 or 12 – no smaller – and sometimes size 8 is better, since the hook needs to be big enough to carry a double wrapping of lead wire or lead foil in several layers under the body dressing, which can be a Pheasant Tail Nymph or similar.

Weight is the key factor, not fly pattern; when trout are feeding near the bottom they usually collect anything that moves, including shrimps, midge larvae and pupae, caddis, damselfly nymphs and snails. They are not fussy.

On many a day the fish may prove difficult to locate and to catch and only as dusk approaches is there a good chance of a fish, and such times are brief – maybe only fifteen minutes or so when the light has gone. Sometimes, during a good evening rise, fish are nearly uncatchable, for some strange reason, and the sole chance of a fish or two to take home comes when the rise has petered out and the surface shows little or no sign of life.

The technique involves fishing with a sink-tip or floating line and either a wake-making Muddler Minnow or a lure, such as a Black Marabou, White Marabou, or Appetiser. The Muddler is cast out as far as possible, from the bank or boat, and then fished back quite slowly, at a speed just fast enough for it to make a little wake. Fish may be seen chasing the fly on the calm surface in the afterglow, but when the splash of the take comes it is folly to tighten immediately, since most fish will be missed or just pricked. Wait until the rod tip becomes heavy with the weight of the fish before lifting firmly.

The white or black lure is also cast a long way, allowed to sink for thirty seconds or so, and then fished as slowly as a nymph. For some strange reason, fish that have been refusing good imitative little flies will take these lures confidently and, when netted, will often be found to have the fly well back in the throat.

There is one other very important peak in the late summer period, and that is when Craneflies (daddy-long-legs) are about on the surrounding grassland and are blown on to the lake by the breeze. With a good imitation well anointed with a flotant on a leader about 10 ft (3 m) long, it is possible to cast to rising fish, or simply to let the fly float for minutes on end until a fish comes up and sucks it down. When fishing the dry fly, do not use a leader that is too long. The resistance of a dry fly in the air, due to its bulk and flared cock hackles, makes it more difficult to cast than a slim-bodied nymph or wet fly. For most dry fly work, a leader 9–12 ft (2.7–3.6 m) long is adequate.

Trout in high mountain lakes do not usually regain good condition until late May or June, and from then until late August is usually the best time for fishing these lonely waters. The fish, wild browns, will not be large – an average weight of 4 oz (115 g) is the norm. However, they fight like 'tame' trout three or more times their size and, because food is in short supply at those altitudes and in the acid water which characterizes them, any flies blown on to the surface are snapped up avidly.

Use the lightest rod and line available – and travel light – because the light tackle will provide maximum enjoyment of the small fish and the absence of heavy gear to carry makes climbing to these lakes, which may take several arduous hours, more bearable. Wild browns in mountain lakes are seldom very selective about fly patterns, and the choice can be limited to three, in sizes 12 and 14: the Pheasant Tail Nymph, leaded and unleaded, the Coch-y-Bondhu and Iron Blue. Alternatives to the two dry flies would be Tup's Indispensable, Grey Duster, Pheasant Tail or Beacon Beige. A light and dark fly give alternative impressions. Though these wild fish are not fussy about fly patterns, they are fussy about leader diameter, and 1½–2 lb (680–900 g) test tippets will catch many more fish than thicker ones. There are always surprises when fishing these high-level waters, and from some in which the fish seldom grow heavier than ½ lb (225 g), the occasional monster of 3–4 lb (1.3–1.8 kg) will surprise the fisherman. A landing net, though seldom used, is a comforting standby in such cases.

Chapter 7
Brown and rainbow trout in rivers

Feeding patterns

Fish location is much easier in river, since fish usually take up lies facing the flow in places where the food-stream is brought to them by the current. However, rivers vary greatly. Some may be gin-clear and smooth-flowing, such as the comparatively placid chalk-streams and limestone rivers found in the English West Country, in Yorkshire, in parts of Ireland, and Normandy, and the limestone streams of the North American continent. Others are brawling torrents, maybe 6 ft (1.8 m) in width, or 100 yd (90 m) wide, or more, cascading their roaring way down mountainsides and through wild moorland.

Watch a rising trout in a river on a late spring or summer day and its rises will often be at regular intervals and in more or less the same place. Such a fish is relatively easy to approach undetected from downstream, since its head is looking upstream, and a competent cast should place the fly upstream of the fish, to drift down and be taken.

Not all river trout feed in such an accommodating manner, however, and on many small streams, particularly on moorland, one has to make constant casts to places where one *expects* fish to be lying, often without a sign of a rise being seen.

Just as in stillwater flyfishing, the dry fly, the nymph and traditional wet flies may be used, in different circumstances. The only method used on still waters that is used very little on rivers is the big lure on a sunken or floating line; but even this technique may be seen in these more englightened times, whereas, a few years ago, such a thing would have been frowned upon. Indeed, it is still frowned upon in some locations: the chalk-

streams, for example, where most of the fishing is limited, by established practice and rules, to dry fly and the upstream imitative nymph only. In wild rivers and streams, on the other hand, the dry fly and nymph are used alongside wet flies; the latter fished singly or in teams of two or three, cast across and allowed to drift down and, maybe, to swing round with the current, until they are downstream of the rod.

When it is possible, the dry fly cast to rising fish is the most enjoyable technique. It is also the easiest of river fishing techniques, for those who can handle the tackle competently and defeat any dragging of the fly (movement of the fly at any speed other than that of the water on which it is borne) by proper line placement and subsequent manipulation.

In clear rivers, whether they be exclusive chalk-streams, moorland becks, or wide, rocky cascades, when a trout can be seen on the fin, lying fairly high in the water and taking the odd fly from the surface, provided the fisherman can gently present a fair likeness in size and colour of the flies the fish is taking, and without being seen – including rod, line and leader – that fish should eventually come to net. It may take patience.

Presentation

Always approach a rising trout or a likely lie very quietly and from downstream, keeping low to prevent silhouette or shadow scaring your quarry; crawl if necessary, and wade quietly if it is permitted. Learn to cast in many ways, so that you are able to get the line flowing out through narrow gaps between trees or almost parallel to the water's surface in those well-bushed corridors of

Wild brown trout from mountain and moorland rivers are usually highly coloured, like this little beauty from the upper Conway in North Wales, or are dark, with rich, red spots.

water so often found on both wild rivers and cultivated chalk rivers. Learn to cast well against the wind, which so often blows strongly downstream, and aim to let the trout see only your fly and fine tippet, never the flyline or any disturbance it may make on the water.

Delicate presentation of line, and fly, or flies, is as important in wet fly and nymph fishing as it is when using the floating fly. In very strong, big rivers it is sometimes best, in order to fish the flies subsurface without any drag furrowing the surface in an unnatural way, to fish with a sinking line. But do not just cast it down and across and let it swing away below you. Fish that take the fly downstream of the rod – on the dangle, as fishermen call it – are often hooked and lost because the angle of the line pulls the fly out of the fish's mouth. It is better, even when using wet flies, to cast slightly upstream and let the flies fish down naturally to only 8 ft (3.6 m) or so below, then lift them off and cast again, preferably moving 1 yd (90 cm) or so downstream each time.

On a tiny river, a rod only 6 ft (1.8 m) long may prove a great advantage in keeping the flyline low and away from the foliage. On a big river, when wet-fly fishing upstream, a long rod – maybe 10 ft (3 m), and lissom – will help pick up the line quickly, so setting the hook into a fast-taking fish. Upstream fishing with the long rod is usually best done with a fairly short length of line out – 15 ft (4.5 m) is often enough. And it should be a light line, too, since its lack of resistance works in just the same way on the river as it does in still water. Hence the lissom rod to cast such a short, light length of line.

Although dry fly fishing is considered to be more fascinating by most fishermen, fishing a sunken nymph to a trout lying 4 ft (1.2 m) or more down, and visible as it swings from side to side to take nymphs and shrimps, is also very absorbing.

In water 4 ft (1.2 m) deep or more, a leaded nymph is often called for in any reasonable flow, but an unleaded nymph may be better in shallower water, or in water that is moving very slowly. The fly has to be cast upstream of the trout, but sink to its level as it approaches the fish. Takes can come to the drifting nymph, but it may be necessary to induce the trout to take by lifting the nymph in the water just as it gets to within 1 ft

(30 cm) or so of the fish. This tactic is very deadly, but not easily done. Both the rod and the hand holding the line must work together to achieve the right motion.

Just as stillwater trout in high, acid mountain lakes tend to accept surface flies when they are available, so do the wild brownies of mountain and moorland rivers that are similarly acid and lacking in the rich insect life of chalk streams and other more alkaline waters. On Exmoor in mid-March the little browns will take dry fly in a snow-storm. One could never get the fish in a chalk-stream to rise with such freedom until May, or when the rich fly-life is beginning to hatch. In chalk-streams, there are rich pickings for the trout on the bottom and in the lush weedbeds.

For dry fly fishing on rivers, the colour of the line does not matter very much: green, brown, white or any other colour will do. The point is, never to let the trout for which you are fishing see the line, no matter what the colour.

The bright orange line – or any other colour that can be seen easily – plays its part in fishing a deep nymph. Most takes will be seen when the fish opens its mouth for the nymph, or swings aside to take it, but sometimes the fish may not be seen very easily, and then the floating part of the leader must be the tell-tale.

In clear rivers, especially chalk-streams, the depth at which the fish feeding on nymphs is lying, is easily underestimated, because of the clarity of the water during the summer, when most nymph fishing is done. Newcomers to such rivers often try to wade in thigh-boots and find themselves waist-deep in water!

Sinking the hook

There are considerable differences between tightening to a trout taking a sunken nymph and doing so to a rise to the dry fly; and again, a difference between the right technique with dry fly on chalk-streams and on fast-flowing rain-fed rivers.

When a chalk-stream trout comes up to accept your dry fly, he is most likely to do so in a leisurely fashion, and once he has it in his mouth – and provided he feels no reason to eject it – he will slowly turn down again and move back to his lie. It is very easy to lift the rod too soon when the fish rises, with the result that the hook is either pulled out of the fish's mouth, or just takes a very light hold in the skin, or bounces off the bony framework of the jaw. It takes great control to wait

that couple of seconds while the fish turns down with the fly before sinking the barb, but that is what must be done if the fish are to be hooked regularly.

On a rain-fed river, especially a small one tumbling down from high ground, trout rise much more quickly to the fast-moving fly, and perhaps because there is more competition for the available food. They are also very adept at ejecting the fly if they feel something is not quite right – and they often do. Therefore, tightening to the take of such trout must be faster, for in addition to the problem of ejection by the fish, the faster current also makes the fish move more quickly to intercept the fly. Many rises on rushing streams are sudden bursts of water; on a slower-flowing, food-rich river, rises tend to be rings, the fly being gently sipped under.

Similarly, in a chalk-stream, when a trout is seen to take the sunken nymph (by being able to watch the actions of the fish or by a signal on the leader), there is a need to tighten quickly – far more quickly than with the floating fly. This is because there is a delay period between the rod tip movement and the subsequent movement of the flyline and the leader angling down into the water. All has to be in a straight – or nearly straight – line before the movement is transmitted to the hook.

To sum up, in slow-moving rivers delay the tightening action with the dry fly but be as fast as you can with the sunken nymph. On fast rivers strike the rise to the floating fly quickly and be just as quick with takes to the wet fly and sunken nymph.

Choice of fly

Just as in stillwaters, fish in rivers can be very choosy at times about the fly they want. This usually happens when there are a number of different flies hatching at the same time, such as in late spring on rain-fed rivers, when various olives (upwing flies) and the Iron Blue are about. The trout's normal preference seems to be for the Iron Blue, and the various olives may be left alone; but the reverse can also be the case.

It is questionable whether it is necessary to carry dozens of different fly patterns to match the various naturals exactly – or as closely as the flydressing art can come. It is possible to be successful using a very limited collection of dry flies, in shades of brown (reddish and ginger), black, buff and grey.

For fishing a nymph or shrimp pattern to fish lying fairly deep, but visible, it is more important to have a pattern that closely copies the naturals. Even so, the Pheasant Tail Nymph, a similar one dressed with grey heron herls instead of cock pheasant centre tail-fibres of rusty hue, and a third of medium olive-green herl will nearly always do the trick.

Most chalk-stream and limestone river fishing does not begin until 1 May – or even a little later – although some rivers open in April. Chalk-stream fishermen, however, prefer to use the dry fly, and since regular rises seldom begin until May, most of them do not start to fish until that lovely month.

By that time, hatches of fly should be quite good, with Medium Olives, Pale Watery Olives and Iron Blues showing well. Black Gnats, a land-bred fly that trout love to take, are also likely to be about.

Unless the Pale Wateries are hatching in profusion, a dark fly is usually the best dry fly choice; something about size 14. Greenwell's Glory, Gold-ribbed Hare's Ear and Iron Blue are good patterns to have, although quite often any small fly of similar colouring will catch fish.

It pays not be be too hidebound about dry fly patterns, even though it is very rewarding to establish what fly the fish are taking, tie on an artificial that looks similar, and find that it works.

A pattern which you should always have with you on a river is Lunn's Caperer, which is supposed to represent a sedge. It has one hackle of black cock and a second of medium Rhode Island Red cock, the body being of brown turkey-tail fibres with a median band of yellow swan herl. It is a bulky fly but it works even when no sedges or look-alike flies are on the water.

Well oiled, the Caperer and any other fuzzy, sedge-imitating pattern can be deadly for trout in smooth, gliding water at dusk, when they are cast almost straight across the current with the line being allowed to belly downstream. The fly is dragged over the surface, making a wake which simulates the wake of a natural sedge-fly trying to take off. Hand-stripping may also be in order, although some chalk-stream purists would frown upon such tactics.

In high summer, when the streams are low and very clear, daytime fishing with the sunk nymph can be quite fascinating. If you are able to 'Indian'

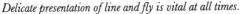

Delicate presentation of line and fly is vital at all times.

to within 5 yd (4.5 m) or so downstream of a good trout hanging near the bottom in 3 ft (90 cm) or more of water, darting from side to side to take nymphs and shrimps swept down by the current or nosing the weeds for them, and can cast a nymph so that it comes down to the fish at his depth, maybe just drifting, maybe lifting before his eyes, it can be very exciting. Every fin-beat, every gill-movement, is visible.

However, while the fish are visible to the fisherman, so are the careless movements of the fisherman to the fish.

Suitable tackle has been discussed in Chapter 2, but there is one point to be made here about fishing small spate streams, and even the feeders and carriers of the chalk-streams. Quite often, the length of flyline one can get outside the rod tip when casting on these tiny streams is only 2 yd

(1.8 m) or so, and that weight of line, if it is matched to the rod in the normal way, is insufficient to flex the rod. One answer is to use a cane rod of 6–7 ft (1.8–2.1 m) with a very easy action. Such a rod performs a casting action, without the weight of a line on it, due to its own weight – something a hollow-glass or graphite rod will seldom do. The alternative is to use a rod for a number 3 with a number 4 or even a 5 line.

For this type of fishing, and for some chalk-stream dry fly work where one casts very few times in a day (and then only to fish seen to rise), the good split-cane rod has a place. Its weight is not excessive in the lengths and for the line sizes used, and the help that the slow, smooth action gives, especially on little streams overgrown with trees, more than compensates for any extra weight on the wrist.

Chapter 8
Seatrout and salmon

Seatrout

Most seatrout flyfishing is done with so-called wet flies, although some of them are more like the reservoir fisherman's lures, including tandem hooks; but the dry fly also works, usually in daylight. The dry fly is also effective when boat fishing on the drift on lakes and lochs holding seatrout, although such floating flies are more often fished by dapping with a rod of 13 ft (3.95 m) or more and a thick but light floss blowline. Effective as these big dry flies are, skittered along the surface with the dapping outfit, it is not really flyfishing, which demands the line be cast rather than blown out by the wind.

Rivers

The flyfisher's seatrout season generally begins in June during warm, settled weather. Fish have begun to move into the rivers and to settle down in the pools. In many rivers seatrout fishing is an after-dark pursuit and few people bother to fish in the daytime.

The night may seem dark to the human eye but to the seatrout it is obviously not. For not only does the seatrout see flies crossing his vision near to the surface while he lies near the riverbed, perhaps 4 ft (1.2 m) or more below, but he can also see a dark, silver-bodied fly at eye level in 6 ft (1.8 m) of water on the blackest night nature ever made.

Big seatrout – fish of 11 lb (5 kg) or more – will run up insignificant little rivers. A stream that is generally less than 3 ft (90 cm) deep and rarely wider than 25 ft (7.5 m) can hold huge fish. But so can rivers that are wide and fast and deep – like the Scottish Spey, for example.

Obviously, with these widely differing river conditions, the flyfishers' tackle must also vary. On a little stream a rod of 8 ft (2.45 m) and a size 5 line might be ideal, whereas on a wide river, where wading is required to cover the water adequately, a rod of 10 ft (3.05 m) and a size 7 line might be needed. The latter outfit would be fine, too, for lough fishing from a boat.

The size of fly being used also affects the rod and line used. A rod of 8 ft (2.45 m) with a size 5 line will be right for a little river when using size 10 traditional wet flies, such as Teal, Blue and Silver, Butcher, Peter Ross, Mallard and Claret, for example. Casting distances may be quite short – maybe never more than 20 ft (6 m). On the other hand, trying to fish a tandem-hooked lure 2½ in (6.5 cm) long near the gravel in a wide pool, where the casting distance is 20 yd (18 m) or more, demands a longer, stiffer rod, a size 7 sinking line and a leader that will not fold up under the weight of the big, air-resistant fly. It is the same story as that of reservoir trout fishing.

Most seatrout flies, wet flies that is, need to be long and slim with plenty of silver tinsel on the bodies and with a dark outline easily seen in silhouette by the fish against the light source.

At night, seatrout tend to move out from under their daytime cover, trees, high banks, rocks and deep holes, and fall back to the smooth-flowing shallow water and the tails of pools. Good fish will be taken in water only 2 ft (60 cm) deep and you should start with a double-taper floating line and one wet fly. Seatrout sometimes accept tiny brown trout flies – size 14 – in daylight, but at night something with more bulk usually does best, and a size 6 or 8 is a good one to start with. A size 4 may do better. Try all three sizes, and drop down to a 10, if you feel the need.

The leader need be no longer than 10 ft (3 m)

Seatrout are wild, vigorous fighters and moments like this, when the fish leaps on the end of a long line, can tear out the hook.

when using a rod of that length; for 8 ft (2.45 m) rod, a leader of 9 ft (2.7 m) will be found reasonable. Because it may be necessary to battle in the dark with a fish of 10 lb (4.5 kg) or more – and many small rivers hold fish of that weight – a tippet of 5–6 lb (2.2–2.7 kg) should be used.

The scheme should entail casting downstream and across, setting the line down as gently as possible, and then letting the flow fish the fly across the river. In slow water it may be necessary to increase the fishing speed of the fly by stripping smoothly with the free hand. Try to make the fly move at the same smooth speed across the river, which may mean stripping it when you feel the tension of the current's pull on the line slackening as the line and fly fish round into your bank.

The floating line will fish the fly between 2 in (5 cm) and 1 ft (30 cm) below the surface, depending on the size (weight) of the fly and current speed. A slim-profile fly is called for, since a bulky fly will tend to be forced to the surface where it will cause a wake. A wake is sometimes attractive to night seatrout, but that is another technique, which will be dealt with later. With the normal wet fly, a subsurface presentation is what is needed. Start at the chosen place at the upstream end of the stretch of water and make at least three casts to the same place from one position before taking a couple of slow, gentle paces downstream. You may be wading thigh-deep or you may be on the bank. No matter what, move with stealth.

Where daytime flyfishing for seatrout is practised, the usual technique is very much like wet fly fishing down and across for brown trout. Smaller flies than are used for night fishing will usually be found more acceptable by the fish and I have had good sport with small fish – 1–2 lb (450–900 g) – using size 14 North Country spider-type trout flies on a floating line.

Still waters

Seatrout fishing in loughs and lochs is usually done from a drifting boat over rocky or gravelly shallow areas and in the region of outflowing and inflowing rivers and feeders. The best areas of each water are known to local anglers and professional gillies and a chat with the first over a drink is never a wasted investment. Good lake (loch/lough) conditions are a south-westerly breeze making a nice ripple on the water, with changing clouds covering intermittent sunshine and maybe the odd warm shower. The boat is drifted beam-on down the wind over recognized seatrout lies

and it may be controlled by the gillie with the oars or with a drogue, depending on the wind strength and the intended path of the boat over the holding ground.

Rods of 10–11 ft (3.05–3.35 m) are customary and usually with a DT6/7 line, which may be a floater, a sink-tip or a sinker. Two flies are usually fished and the dropper is brought back to dibble the surface near the boat, just as in lake fishing for brown trout. Sometimes seatrout will be seen to rise, just like brown trout, and such movements should be covered quickly and the flies fished quite fast over the spot.

Provided there is a ripple, the wind that makes it can be relatively unimportant: some lakes fish well in a northerly or north-westerly breeze. Easterly winds are not conducive to good fishing as a rule – but rules are often thrown aside.

Estuaries

Both in the river and on lakes, the seatrout that take most frequently are those which have been in freshwater the shortest time. It therefore seems obvious that if we fish for them in the sea – or in an estuary – our chances are better than in freshwater. And in many places, such is the case.

While in saltwater, seatrout feed heavily on sand-eels, small fish such as sprats and herring fry, shrimps and prawns. The best flies for use in saltwater or brackish estuarine water, therefore, are those that look like sand-eels, small fish or shrimps and prawns – lures, in fact, from 2½–3½ in (6.5–9 cm) in length.

Both rocky, weedy estuaries and shallow, sandy ones can produce seatrout and since long casting may be called for, and because we need to make our lures appear like small fish or crustaceans darting through the water among the rocks, weeds and over the sand, we can strip them, just like in stillwater trout fishing with the lure. And that indicates the need to use a weight-forward or shooting-taper line, a floater, maybe, or a sink-tip or full sinker, depending on the depth of the water and its flow.

Night fishing also produces good sport in saltwater, but be very careful not to wade too deeply or get cut off by a flooding tide. Another hazard is that of getting a foot trapped between rocks. Try to fish from the shore or marginal shallows in the darkness rather than risk an accident. However, in some shallow, sandy estuaries, wading at night can be fairly safe, provided a weather-eye is kept on the tide. While the latter half of the ebb tide and

With plenty of room between them, the two salmon fishermen work down Hafod Pool of the Gwydyr Hotel water of the Conway near Betws-y-Coed in North Wales.

the low water period is generally most productive, there are places where the fish only move into range towards high water. Such places include tiny bays with streams running into them or even long inlets on salt marshes.

A final point about catching seatrout in the sea: no seatrout you catch in the river will have such beauty, such a wonderful shape, will fight so hard. Seatrout from saltwater have a silver, lilac, dark blue and pinkish glow about them that is never found in a fish in the river, even taken low down when it has been in freshwater only a few hours.

Salmon

Salmon fishing is a world apart. It is different from all other types of angling because the Atlantic salmon, *Salmo salar*, does not feed in freshwater. The fact that a salmon will take into its mouth a bunch of live worms, a long-dead prawn or shrimp, a wooden, plastic or metal spinner, or other lure, or an angler's artificial fly, is something

not far short of a miracle. It is also a miracle that a salmon may swim up a river in January and spawn in November when the year is dying, and do so without having eaten anything at all in the eleven months between.

Tackle

Once again, the size of the fly being used, the depth at which it must be fished and the strength of the stream dictate the tackle used. In the cold, heavy water of February to mid-April, and again, to a slightly lesser extent, in October and November, a heavy sinking line is needed to push out the big, heavy, air-resistant fly and cast it 25 yd (22.8 m) or more, and to take it down to fish deep in the flow. Number 9, 10 and 11 double-taper lines are customary for this style of fishing and to cast them, and the fly, and to be able to control them in the water and lift them off again for the next cast, a very powerful, long rod is necessary. Even on comparatively small rivers – averaging perhaps 25 yd (22.8 m) across – a 14 ft (4.25 m) rod and a line of at least size 9 would be chosen. On bigger rivers with strong flows, like the Tay or Spey, the line might need to be size 11 and the rod 17 ft (5.1 m) long.

Rod length serves a number of useful purposes. In casting, using the normal overhead cast with two hands instead of one, the heavy line and big fly are kept well above the fisherman's head, helping to prevent nasty accidents: a 3 in (6.5 cm) fly dressed on a length of brass tube with a treble hook at its tail-end, propelled by the heavy line (the combined weight of fly and line might be nearly 2 oz (60 g)) can cause bad wounds to the head and neck on the forward cast! The high line cast by the long rod also helps keep the fly clear of vegetation, high banks or rocks behind the caster, and it also helps make special casts, such as the Spey- or roll-cast, in which the line does not pass behind the angler, much easier.

And when the line and fly is fishing around across the current, holding the long rod out over the water helps to decrease the angle of the line to the current, thereby slowing down the fly's progress, which is desirable.

Rod length and weight must, of course, be selected by the fisherman to suit his physical abilities. Casting a very long rod and holding it out over the river can cause a great deal of strain on the arms, shoulders and back muscles. A big, strong man may find a 17 ft (5.10 m) graphite rod just the job, whereas a smaller man, a boy, or a

Salmon like to lie in shadow, if they can, and suitable flow beneath trees, under bridges, high rocks and other natural and man-made features is always worth trying.

woman, might find a 13 ft (3.95 m) about as much as he or she can cope with. Good hollow-glass salmon rods from 12–15 ft (3.65 m to 4.55 m) are very good, although they are not so light as graphite and have other disadvantages. One of these is the fact that the rod needs to be fairly thick in section, and this creates wind resistance when casting, adding to the required effort, and when a wind is blowing up or down the river, even holding the rod out against wind pressure can be exhausting.

Split-bamboo rods, specially the ones where the sections are joined by splicing rather than by metal ferrules are still popular and fish very well indeed. Up to 14 ft (4.25 m) they are manageable by any reasonably strong person, provided an occasional rest is taken after fishing a pool, and the splices do not tend to loosen and turn, causing misalignment of the rings, as metal ferrules do during the twisting stresses involved in roll-casting, and so on.

Salmon are very strong fish and even a fish of

8 lb (3.6 kg) can take the whole line and 60 yd (55 m) or more of backing from the reel in a strong downstream run in fast water. Therefore, with the thickness of heavy lines, plus the need for at least 100 yd (90 m) of 20–25 lb (9–11.3 kg) test braided Terylene backing, a reel to hold it comfortably so that, even when it has been wound on hurriedly without being neatly spread across the spool, the level of the line will be clear of the reel's crossbars and not cause jams, is necessary. Most salmon flyreels have a diameter of at least 4 in (10 cm), maybe 4½ in (11.5 cm), although some, with wide spools, may have a diameter of 3½ in (9 cm).

Reels should have good, strong checkwork and, preferably, some form of adjustment on the strength of the check or drag.

Salmon may be landed by hand-tailing, getting a good grip round the firm wrist of the fish's tail with the thumb and forefinger towards the tail, but this is only possible where the fish can be played out and picked up from shallow, slack water. Doing so while holding up a long flyrod is no easy task, and a partner is the best answer. Salmon can also be beached, but again, this depends on whether the river has suitable, shallow sloping spots, which some do not. The single-handed salmon fisherman is better off with a gaff or a tailer.

Leaders for salmon fishing need not usually be tapered: a length of level nylon cut straight from a spool is normally sufficient, and 8 lb (3.5 kg) test is about right for most fishing in the April–September period, with 12–15 lb (5.5–6.7 kg) for sunk-line work with big flies. On rare occasions in summer, when the river runs very low and gin clear and when size 12 doubles or single-hook flies down to size 10, or a ½ in (12 mm) tubefly with a size 14 treble hook, may be the only sure way of attracting takes, a knotless-tapered leader to about 6 lb (2.7 kg) test might be an advantage, not only for delicate presentation but to permit the nylon to pass easily through the tiny hook eyes.

Salmon fishing

The basis of salmon fishing with the fly is a very simple one. It is to cast the flyline across and slightly downstream of one's position, and allow it to swing across the flow fairly slowly, with the fly on its almost invisible leader following it, sinking and lifting, fluttering its delicate dressing of feather-fibres and hairs in the vagaries of the current as it does so. That the fly may fish within 1 in (2.5 cm) or so of the surface or within 1 ft (30 cm)

or so of the riverbed is simply a variation in level.

This action of the fly, be it a big, colourful fly in cold, powerful water in February or March, or a tiny drab one on a hot July day, is attractive to the salmon, which swims up to intercept its movement and take it. Usually a salmon takes a fly very deliberately, holding it in its mouth and returning from whence it came – to its lie. In most cases, striking at the take of a salmon as one does to a trout taking a nymph or wet fly, is incorrect.

With a sunk line in cold water the take is usually felt as a sudden strong pull and the instinctive reaction is to pull back. And this is correct in this case, since the fly has been taken deep, or fairly so, in the water, and usually with a fair length of line out, which is how the fly fishes most deeply, dragged down by the heavy sinking line. And the line will usually have a bow in it as it swings across the stream, which is partially straightened by the pull of the fish as it takes the fly and swings back to its lie. All this takes time, albeit only a second or less, and it is enough for a simple firm lifting of the rod, preferably sideways and up rather than in a perpendicular direction, away from the direction of the pull, to sink the barb in the side of the salmon's jaw.

One hears advice to let the salmon take line from the reel before tightening, but few fishermen can control their reactions in the excitement of the moment, should the truth be known. One also hears of holding about 1 yd (90 cm) of slack line between reel and butt ring, letting it go when the pull is felt before lifting the rod. But a loop of line in such a place is often the cause of tangles, and you should have no problem with hooking fish on the sunk line and big fly, if you lift and hold the line firmly against the cork handle with the upper hand.

Fishing in warmer water and weather conditions, with the floating or sink-tip line and with the fly fishing 1 in (2.5 cm) subsurface, or maybe as deep as 1 ft (30 cm) in slower water, the situation at the take is quite different. Often, the fish is seen to come to the fly, head and back breaking surface as it takes, before it goes down again. Or the boil of the fish taking a little deeper will be seen, and the line will suddenly tighten.

It is tempting to strike immediately, and this is wrong, because the line that is floating, or mainly lying on the surface, transmits to the angler what is happening at the fly end of his tackle much more quickly than when the line is deep in the water, bellying downstream, and the fish invisible. And in any case, in summer conditions, the angler will try to control his floating line so that no down-stream belly – or excessive belly at any rate – forms, dragging his fly across the stream more quickly than is usually desirable. The floating line can be *mended*, lifted upstream by a slow, circular movement of the rod, both immediately after the cast has been made and during the line's travel across the river. This avoids the fast current that often flows between the angler and where his fly is fishing, dragging the intermediate line down-stream faster than the tip.

A sunken line cannot be thus controlled, although it often pays to mend the line immedi-ately the cast has been made and before the line has been able to sink very far, to allow the line to gain depth before the intervening current gets hold of it.

So, with the fly high in the water and the floating/sink-tip line, a degree of delay in tighten-ing is desirable. It permits the fish time to take the fly, close its mouth, and begin to turn away and down to its lie again. A pull by the fisherman at

that moment, with the fish facing away from him and maybe turning its head downstream, will pull the hook *back* into the jaw. An early tightening may pull the fly out of the salmon's mouth before the mouth has closed, or even if it has closed, a pull from directly or slightly upstream can pull the fly *forward* and out of the mouth.

For these reasons, then, a take on the fly being fished high in the water should be delayed, and the metre of line between reel and butt ring serves to make this possible. The line is let go until it tight-ens, and then the answering pull is given.

Some fishermen are incapable of such self-control and for them it is best to fish with the reel on a light drag or check tension, and without holding the line at all. When the take comes, he must wait until he hears the line begin to leave the reel, and only then should he tighten up.

There are occasions when, instead of trying to avoid a belly in the floating line – and thus fishing the fly too quickly across a fast current – the fisherman either tries to create a slight down-stream belly or actually strips line in with his free hand, rather like fishing a reservoir fly or lure, to make the fly fish faster. Such instances occur when fishing slow water in which salmon are known to be lying but in which more life than the current

These two fish took a size 10 low water fly from the same pool, and there were two other fine fish in the bag at the end of the day.

will give is needed to fish the fly in an attractive manner. Remember, the salmon was chasing his food in the sea and it is the moving object that attracts him. A fly simply drifting lifelessly down the river is very unlikely to attract a fish.

Today, far too many fishermen mend line far too often, and frequently for no good reason. On most salmon pools the line may be cast at such an angle that, apart from an immediate mend, to allow the fly to sink a little before the line begins to drag it across, no mending at all is necessary as the fly comes across. Holding the long rod out over the water, and with its tip high, to keep as much of the line near the angler as possible off any faster water than that in which the fly is fishing, helps to fish the fly across slowly.

When stripping the fly to give it life as it slowly crosses slow-moving water, the take is likely to be very similar to that of a stillwater trout on a lure: a sudden hard pull. And since the fisherman is pulling line, too, the hook is likely to penetrate the fish's jaw at the instant it takes – or it will not get a hold at all.

Once a fish is hooked, play it from the reel. Keep the rod high, well bent and move around to keep abreast or slightly downstream of your fish. Stay upstream when a fish runs down, and when you put strain on him again you will be pulling the hook towards the front of the fish's mouth – and maybe out of it. Keep as much of the heavy flyline as possible out of the water. The drag of the line can break the leader if the fish moves fast enough to create a big bow in the sunken line.

Having said that the basis of salmon fishing is simple, it is also true that skill is demanded: to decide where fish might be resting; to fish the right fly at the right depth and the right speed; to play and secure the fish. However, in the long run, persistence is the real key to salmon-fishing success; that, and an eye for the water. Try to get your mind to wriggle its way down the line to your fly as you fish. Imagine what the fly is doing, and what any salmon may be doing, too. Take trouble; take time. Fish every yard of the water; if you come to trees lining your bank, do not walk around them just because casting will be a problem. If possible – and this goes for a high bank behind, or a cliff, too – wade in and roll-cast your way past the hazard behind. Others may have taken the easy way out and left a fish there for you.

Chapter 9
Grayling

Grayling cannot tolerate water that is warm or polluted; it is far more susceptible in both these respects than the trout or the salmon. Cool, clean, fast-flowing water is what the grayling has to have, and if those conditions change, the grayling tends to migrate upstream, where the water is likely to be more pure. Many of today's rivers that held grayling almost from source to mouth a few years ago, now have them only in their head-waters.

Grayling live on a diet of mainly freshwater shrimps and nymphs of varied water-bred flies, although they like to eat worms, maggots and even the breadbaits of coarse fishermen. They are at their best in the period from September until after Christmas, and even in October and November, they may be taken on the fly, both sunken and floating, when the water is clear and the weather mild.

Grayling tend to swim in shoals of half-a-dozen to more than fifty fish. They like fairly shallow, gravel-bottomed areas where the water flows smoothly, although they will also lie in deep, eddying pools in the dead of winter. Although they are just as easily scared as trout, by a heavy footfall, or a silhouette, or shadow falling over them, they are easier to catch than trout. Fish after fish may be taken from the same shoal, provided you do not let the hooked fish splash about too much, but drag it downstream and away from its fellows. Also, grayling will rise repeatedly to a dry fly, missing it several times but then taking it firmly on, perhaps, the tenth attempt.

Scare a shoal and they will scatter, up or down the river, but providing you kneel quietly out of sight, they are most likely to return to the spot within five minutes, and are then immediately catchable again.

Tackle

Light trout tackle, as suitable for dry fly and nymph on small rivers, is fine for grayling fishing, but err on the light side, using a double-taper size 3 or 4 floating line and a very flexible matching rod of 8½–9 ft (2.60–2.75 m), since the fast strikes needed to hook them are better cushioned with such a rod.

The fishing is far more enjoyable if you can see the fish in the river, and the clearer rivers, especially the crystalline chalk-streams, are best. North of England rivers often colour up with rain and make visual fishing impossible, although casting a dry fly to the rising fish is then a profitable and enjoyable technique. Provided the water remains clear, which is often the case on the chalk-streams, grayling may be spotted in the river even in the dead of winter, and they may still be caught on a leaded, deeply-sunk nymph.

Dry fly fishing

There are special dry flies for grayling, most of them rather fat-bodied affairs with just a hackle, no wing and, often, a short tail of silk of feather fibre, red or yellow. They have names like Red Tag, Treacle Parkin, Green Insect, and various Bumbles. But grayling are not fastidious. They will take almost any small trout fly, and sizes 14 and 16 are generally the most acceptable.

The best of all dry fishing for grayling comes in September and throughout the warm days of October, when there are still good numbers of various flies to attract them to surface-feed, and shallow, swift water only 2 ft (60 cm) deep over gravel produces excellent sport. The fish can be located with polarizing glasses and, with careful fishing, fish after fish may be taken. With the characteristically small flies that the grayling prefer, a thin leader tippet – about 2 lb (900 g) test – is called for, and I have known fish accept a fly gleefully on that but turn away from the same pattern on a 3 lb (1.3 kg) tippet.

Unlike trout, however, grayling are not put off

Late summer and autumn grayling fishing with the fly, both dry and sunken nymph, is excellent sport in colourful surroundings.

by a dry fly that creates a certain amount of drag; indeed, some drag is very often more attractive to the grayling than a fly floating down perfectly drag-free.

Although grayling are never as fussy about the exact copy of the fly that is hatching most profusely, and which they are mainly feeding on, as are trout, they can sometimes be quite selective. This selective feeding occurs more when there are heavy hatches of Pale Watery Olives or, in October more than in September, Large Dark Olives.

Also unlike trout, grayling will shoal in open, shallow reaches of the river where there is little cover in the form of weeds or overhanging foliage. Their camouflage, though, is often excellent, and it can take time to locate them. The fish in one shoal are usually all about the same size, and if your first casts produce fish of around 8 oz (450 g), it is unlikely, but not impossible, that you will catch bigger fish in that place.

Grayling may be caught by wet fly fishing downstream and across, casting to cover the river at random and working downstream, but just as with all fish that take the fly fished downstream, many fish will be hooked momentarily and then shake free. The angle of pull is all wrong. But many fish are caught each year in this way, and small spider-type flies work well.

Nymph fishing

Nymph fishing is the best sport of all with grayling. The water may be only 2 ft (60 cm) deep, or less, or up to 4 ft (1.2 m) or more, but provided the fish have been located, great bags may be taken.

Either the Pheasant Tail Nymph or Sawyer's Killer Bug could be successful, with plenty of lead under the dressings for water 4 ft (1.2 m) deep or more, and for water that is less than that depth but flowing briskly. It is a real problem to get the nymph down to the fish lying on the bottom, and they seem to like it when it is actually trundling along the gravel. Grayling should be played gently in fast water, for they can pull very hard indeed, and they can either bend or break the tiny hooks used.

Chapter 10
Tackle

At one extreme, there's the man who takes everything with him on a fishing trip – just in case. At the other, there's the guy who carries a minimum of gear, sometimes even relying on others to fill any gaps that become apparent later. While the former approach often turns out to be a masochistic form of weight-training, the latter is practical only after years of experience.

The middle road is followed by the angler who hedges his bets efficiently. There is a limit to the number of species likely to be found at any mark selected for a day's fishing, so a few extra items of tackle allow different methods to be employed without adding much to one's burden. If the frustrated crab fisher had packed a few spinners or red-gill sand-eels he would have arrived home with a smug grin of satisfaction, and wouldn't have kicked the cat.

Obviously much of what one takes on a fishing trip depends on what is expected, and this comes with experience. Even so, research will reveal what to expect on a trip to a strange shore. Charts, maps, phone-calls to tackle dealers and a dollop of common sense will slim down the load of gear required to cover every eventuality.

Rods

The only rods worth using are built from glass-reinforced plastic or glass/carbon-reinforced plastic. No rods are built exclusively of carbon (also called graphite) because at present such a rod would snap. Glass fibre is required for lateral strength in a carbon rod. Glass is a heavier material than carbon, so rods built from it are heavier and thicker than those built with carbon.

Top shore fishermen prefer fast-action rods because they are better for long casting and have fine tips that show up bites well. The middle section of a fast rod is flexible enough to absorb the lunges of hooked fish and thereby prevent a taut line from being shock-loaded to breaking point. Rods used in high-velocity casting have totally rigid butts, as this is more efficient at transmitting casting energy to the rod-tip, causing the sinker to fly out faster and therefore further.

A good rod will have its reel fitting some 28 in (70 cm) up from the butt cap. In the old days this distance – or 'reach' – used to be some 36 in (90 cm) or more, resulting in abysmal casting technique. Some good casters prefer to hold the reel a few inches up from the butt even though such a position inevitably increases the leverage a hooked fish imposes on an angler.

Blanks are now so delicate and precise that they should not be hobbled – crippled, even – through using inferior fitments on them.

Rod length for efficient casting need be no more than 11½ ft (3.50 m). Such a weapon is ideal for all styles of casting, including the pendulum style, although several experts who practise the less common South African and Yarmouth styles prefer slightly longer rods. But a long rod imposes leverage against the caster and many shore anglers over-rod themselves in the mistaken belief that extra length produces extra casting distance. In one sense it does. Extra length compensates for inefficient casting technique and poor style, but even so this advantage is very slender when compared to the results achieved by a practised performer of a powerful, efficient casting style like the pendulum when using the 11½ ft (3.50 m) rod. Some anglers argue that a long rod holds line above the water, away from plucking breakers and weed floating close in. Well, a shorter, lighter rod can be held with the tip high or put to rest in a long monopod rod-rest, thus achieving the best of both arguments.

Local custom and fishing conditions often dictate the rod to use. The man who frequently fishes for congers from piers is likely to prefer a much shorter rod. Those who fish the rocky shores of Yorkshire frequently employ rods that are extremely stiff, using them to winch tackle free of weed and boulder jungles or to hoist a fish up the side of a cliff.

For most British shore anglers, where 4–6 oz (120–180 g) sinkers are needed to carry a big bait aloft or to push out a very long way, such a rod as outlined earlier will be quite adequate. This is the heavy artillery, for use when fishing for cod, conger, rays, tope and so on. It is at home on both piers and open shoreline. The angler who needs to cast lighter sinkers can buy a slimmer version to handle 3–4 oz (90–120 g) sinkers. And the bass specialist will find that an even slimmer version that casts 2–3 oz (60–90 g) sinkers will cope with virtually every bass-fishing situation – and several others where bass are not the quarry.

Modern blanks cope with a wide range of weights. Even so, they work best within a narrow loading band. Thus the big stick will cast a 5–6 oz (150–180 g) sinker and a couple of lugworms like a rocket up to a possible 200 yd (200 m). The same rod couldn't cast a 7 oz (210 g) sinker that far because it would be overloaded, while a 4 oz (120 g) sinker wouldn't load the rod sufficiently to draw out its full potential. The limit is reached when a rod is loaded to excess by a combination of too much bait, too heavy a sinker and too powerful a casting style. Under extreme conditions it will snap. A rod can be overloaded if an angler holds it in an upright position while pulling out of a snag. This causes plenty of rods to snap each year. When snagged, reel in line until the rod is pointing along the line, then pull directly against the obstruction with all the pressure on the reel. Or, if heavy line is used, wind the line round a piece of wood so as to take the strain off both rod and reel.

Other rods will prove useful. You can get a spinning rod or two. While the bass rod is also ideal for paternostering a spinner, a proper spinning rod adds an extra dimension of sensitivity to a form of fishing that is often only as successful as the angler is skilful – in greater proportion than is the case with some other methods.

A reservoir-style fly rod rated for AFTM 9–10 lines can be employed to good effect in some areas, while a 13 ft (3.95 m) freshwater match angler's rod is suitable not only for mullet fishing, but also for casting out light sinkers for whiting, pouting, school bass and flatfish where conditions and tides permit such a sporting approach. Again, carbon/glass blanks make the strongest, lightest and slimmest weapons.

Today's glass and carbon rods are easy to maintain. The only damage likely to occur is scarring, through dropping them or letting them fall on to the beach or similar hard surfaces; the occasional broken ring (once more common, when tungsten carbide or welded stainless steel rings were used);

and the inevitable scratching of varnish. All rods profit by the occasional wash. Care should be taken to keep sand from ferrules, where it will grind away at the material.

Reels

Most shore fishermen prefer a multiplier reel for heavy work and a fixed-spool for spinning and mullet fishing. Some models of fixed-spool are designed for heavy work, but with modern rods becoming even lighter, such hefty reels are cumbersome. By comparison, multipliers are more compact, more adaptable, and more efficient.

A problem experienced by the tyro when learning to use a multiplier is variously known as a bird's-nest, over-run, back-lash and, ultimately, a crack-off or frapp-off. This condition is caused by the reel spool spinning faster than the flying sinker can drag line out through the rod-rings, or by failure on the angler's part to brake the spool when the tackle hits water, and is usually due to a combination of incompetence and optimism. Multipliers should never be tuned up so that they are totally free-running. However, anglers with poor casting styles frequently ignore all the controls of line flow built into a reel, in the hope that the sinker will fly out further. A really good crack-off leaves the spool looking like a nylon hedgehog with loose ends poking out from a mass of twisted coils. Such a one requires surgery, cutting back to sound line. Don't lose your temper and tug savagely at the mess or matters will deteriorate. Always inspect line very carefully after a snarl-up and cut off any that shows signs of damage.

Adequate braking is achieved by the use of one or two brake-blocks, according to one's ability. A less consistent method is the use of heavy oil in spindle bearings. As an extreme measure, the spool's spindle can be squeezed by tightening the bearing cap at one end.

Spool-braking control is vital when casting large air-resistant baits that cause the sinker to decelerate rapidly. Indeed, it is sometimes necessary to keep a thumb feathering the spool during the cast for extra control.

When those extra yards are not necessary, a level-wind is a boon, spooling back line evenly, permitting the angler to concentrate exclusively on playing and landing the fish. When a level-wind is not used, there are times when the thumb is not so efficient and mounds and hollows appear. Just lob out and rewind evenly, else a crack-off is

Time for contemplation.

Fly-fishing for estuary bass is hectic when schoolies shoal up at dusk during high summer.

guaranteed for your next cast.

A feature of both fixed-spool reels and multipliers is a drag system that allows fish to take line at a tiring pressure. The fixed-spool also allows the angler to knock off the anti-reverse catch and back-wind the handle, playing the fish through the gears rather than using the slipping clutch. When fishing for non-fighters like cod, many anglers keep the drag screwed up fairly tight, loosening it only when the fish is close in and a sudden lunge wouldn't be absorbed by the elasticity of the line or rod tip. While landing a fish, it is wise to back the drag right off, applying any necessary pressure to the spool with a thumb or finger. This sensitive approach allows instant reaction to a sudden, panicky run or surging wave that might break the line.

Another feature of multipliers is a click mechanism that is used to warn that a fish is running with the bait. This is ideal for some forms of fishing where takes come with long intervals in between, or a fish needs to be allowed to run some way with a bait before it will take it properly. If tidal pressure causes the click to signal false takes, put the reel into gear, but wind off the drag to a point where the tide doesn't take line. This is the only method that can be used with a fixed-spool. No matter what, it is unwise to let a fish feel the check. The extra drag may spook it. So knock the reel into free spool and gingerly thumb the spool to prevent an over-run.

A word on fighting fish. At no time should it be allowed to snap the line – a sure sign of either a monster or of incompetence. Keep the rod tip high and use the rod tip and drag pressure to both cushion lunges and tire it out. However, when fishing for cod or other species that allow the angler to reel them in without registering protest until they're close to the beach, wrist strain is prevented by pointing the rod along the line and reeling it in as waves push the fish towards you. Be prepared to change methods the moment it takes fright.

When a big fish or weed exerts pressure, pump it in: wind down until the rod points along the line, then drag the fish in a few feet by raising the rod tip high. Reel in as you drop the rod tip again, and so on. An alternative is to walk backwards up the beach, reeling in while walking back down to the water's edge.

A reel is a precision instrument. A multiplier spool spins in excess of 20,000 RPM during a high-velocity cast. Careful maintenance will guarantee longevity. Disregard for reel maintenance costs both fish, through drags freezing at moments of stress, and money, through excessive wear.

Line

Nylon monofilament line is the only type worth using from the beach. Braided Terylene or Dacron (the same, but different brand names) can be used where extra sensitivity to bites is required, but it abrades easily and needs a nylon leader to take the worst of the punishment.

Line is the only link between angler and fish. It must be strong, with no nicks and abrasions. Even so, cheap-skates skimp on line, making do with worn-out stuff, then grizzle when specimens break free.

Remember that the sea-bed is abrasive, and that spool-slip may singe line while casting. Heavy wear also comes from landing several fish or hauling lumps of weed – which is also abrasive. Spool off old line for casting practise.

Nylon absorbs water. Knots also reduce its strength by a combined total of around 10 per cent. If a knot fails to snug up neatly, cut if off and retie. Lines should be spooled on tightly to within $\frac{1}{8}$ in (3 mm) of the lip of the spool. Over-loaded reels produce tangles and bird's-nests, so don't be tempted to put on just a few extra yards to compensate for line lost due to wear during the first sessions of its life. It's not worth the trouble. Too little line is bad for casting and reduces the effectiveness of modern highly-geared reels, which, with small spools, require a full complement of line for efficiency. After a heavy session, make a few casts with just a sinker, retrieving line before it sinks in the water. Run it through a rag to remove dirt and it will then be ready for use next trip. Or wind it off at home, letting it dry before re-spooling. Never let *oil* get on line, or squirt WD40 and similar on to loaded reels.

Where light line is desirable but heavy sinkers are required, knot on a casting leader (also known as a shock leader) to take the force of the cast. Leaders are also useful for controlling big fish awaiting the drop net while pier fishing and when a big fish needs to be dragged from surf on very steep beaches. A leader need be no longer than twice the length of the rod (for casting) and in strength – well, this depends on what you're doing with it. A useful formula is to allow 10 lb (4.5 kg) of test strength for 1 oz (30 g) of sinker. Thus a 5 oz

When bottom fishing among rugged territory, you have to accept high losses of hooks and sinkers.

(150 g) sinker requires a 50 lb (22.5 kg) shock leader.

There are two severe flaws in line. Firstly, shredding, when the outer skin breaks away, leaving the line feeling like twine, and secondly, excessive stretch, which builds up pressure that will crush, burst or distort reel spools. Line used for leaders should be the soft variety. Wiry leaders are an abomination. However, too soft line weakens quickly.

There is little to choose between various makes of line. Price is a reliable guide. Anglers who swear by one line express prejudice about another make that somebody else uses all the time. Some people are happy to use cheap, bulk line that others abhor. The only guidance worth following is this: find a make of line that you like, and stick to it. More is gained from familiarity with the characteristics of one specific make, than from wide experimentation with different makes.

Other items of gear

Rod rests are vital at times. On rocks, use a tripod if there aren't suitable, natural rod rests about. On penetrable shorelines, use a monopod.

Always buy good hooks, and sharpen them with a small triangular file. Smear the file with silicone grease to prevent rust, which will blunt it. Match hook size to bait and fish species pursued. Use strong hooks, but not heavy ones where thick metal is a substitute for inferior design or temper.

Swivels are rarely necessary to eliminate twist from nylon, except when spinning. Their main function is as links between items of terminal gear. The strongest are those with the wire loop entering the swivel body in the shape of an omega, or, in recent designs, a triangulated omega. Split-rings can be used instead of swivels. They are cheaper, less reliable, and more fiddly to tie on.

A small essential item is a lead-clip. This prevents line knotted to a lead's eye from banging against stones while being retrieved. This damages the join, and is the most common reason for nylon snapping at that point, which can be exceedingly dangerous in mid-cast. Lead-clips are cheap to buy, cheap to make and should always be used if the sinker isn't to be sacrificed.

Bait-clips prevent baits from flapping about and ensure perfect bait presentation. They can be made from old flex cover and stainless steel wire. Clips can be used where long traces are employed, because the hook trace can be tied to the leader several feet up from the sinker, such a knot slipping easily through the rod rings.

Lighting can be provided by electric torches, or a head-lamp that can be bought with a battery pack. The best power sources are rechargeable Nicad cells, or a six-volt motor-bike battery, which can be recharged cheaply. Keep the latter in a polythene bag, held with elastic bands, in case of acid leaks. Paraffin pressure lamps are standard equipment nowadays. Pack them carefully – glasses become fragile with age. An extendable pole to hold the lamp high above the beach maximizes its efficiency. Even so, it is wise to paint rod-tops white or fluorescent yellow, or fit reflective tape over the top 18 in (45 cm).

A coarse angler's umbrella is useful, with or without a draught-excluding sheet of polythene. Anchor brollies well, with a stake buried in shingle, or with the crown tied via a length of rope to a canvas bag filled with stones or sand.

Use grapnel leads where very strong tides are encountered, as breakaway and other release-type leads don't work in severe currents. Bead-type breakaway leads are patent and are available in most shops. Apart from a range of major sinkers, like 5 and 6 oz (150 and 180 g) grapnels and 2–5 oz (60–150 g) release leads, you'll need drilled bullets for floats, split shot also for floats, and small bombs for light legering.

Terminal rigs

Contrary to what some believe, the fish are not impressed by complicated rigs. Provided heavy wire booms are not used – and some anglers still use them, terrible though they are – most rigs can

be built from well-knotted nylon, one or two swivels, a lead-clip, a hook or two and some lead. How many hooks? As a general rule, one hook is adequate when the fish are feeding. The important ingredient is the carefully-prepared bait. Terminal rigs are judged on their effectiveness at presenting the bait unobtrusively and at keeping the rodster informed of what is happening.

Running paternoster This is rigged so that the sinker precedes the bait. Even a ¾ oz (22 g) bomb will therefore lead a big crab out to the fishing area. It is an excellent rig that doesn't tangle. The fish can take line and give good bite indication where water pressure on line between the swivels and the angler doesn't muffle

Grip leads. Bead breakaway 1. ready for use and 2. collapsed; elastic band break-out lead, 3. ready for use and 4. collapsed; 5. grapnel lead with in-built bait clip.

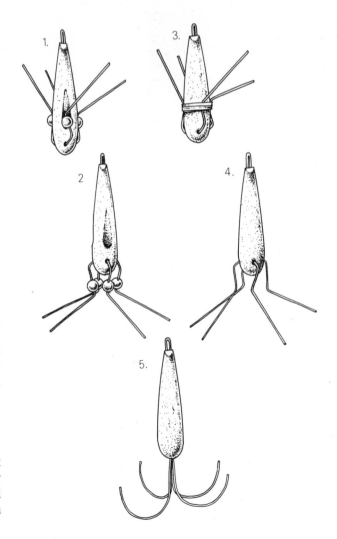

this, as happens in long-range casting, when a fixed paternoster is more effective. Ensure the two swivels are of the same size, else the eye of one will jam in the eye of the other.

Fixed paternoster This is standard for all long-range fishing, because it is so streamlined. The free swivel rotates in any direction, thus preventing a small fish from tangling the trace when spinning in the tide.

Basic leger rig This is simple, and useful for many types of fishing. If you like long traces (which tend to tangle, don't catch any more fish, muffle bite detection, and tend to catch around rock and weed stems) this is the best rig to use. In snaggy ground, tie a couple of inches of weaker line between sinker and swivels, but remember that this action prevents full-blooded casting – the lead will fly off.

Basic float rig No problem here. The float need be no more than a small piece of polystyrene, tied round with old nylon ending in a small swivel to run on the line. Cheap and easy to lose when wrasse fishing in snaggy areas – standard wrasse country.

Spinning paternoster More efficient than putting lead on the trace above the lure. This tends to drag the lure into snags. But the paternoster hampers seductive action to a lesser degree, while weak line to the sinker allows you to break free from obstructions and maybe not lose the lure. The addition of a boom sometimes prevents tangling, though it is rarely needed.

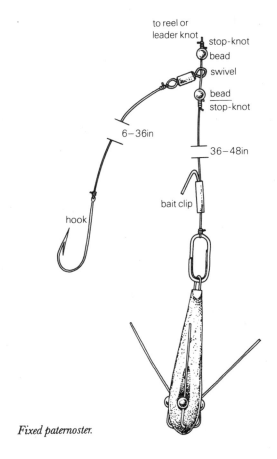

Fixed paternoster.

Running paternoster.

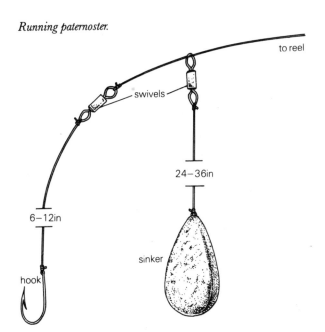

Basic leger rig.

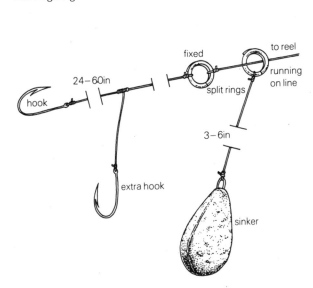

Casting

There are several different styles of cast used around British coasts. Least powerful of all is the overhead thump, as practised by the majority of shore anglers. This style uses little more than the arms to put speed into the rod. It is excellent for accuracy, poor for distance.

Next there are the various styles of lay-back cast. These provide moderate distance, are adequately accurate, and are powered by the arms and the caster's shoulders. Swivelling of the trunk also adds some steam.

Then there are the three high-velocity styles. First, and most popular, is the pendulum style. Less widespread is the South African style, and the Yarmouth back-swing is used mainly by casters around the shallow East Anglian shore. These three long-range styles owe much to the fact that they employ the full body power of the caster, starting from the balls of the feet, flowing through the entire body to the arms. It is this more than anything else that makes high-velocity casting look so graceful and effortless, especially when compared to the strenuous, unscientific antics of those fishermen who attempt to stretch the overhead thump style to distances that it cannot reach.

Long-range casting enables the shore angler to reach distant hot-spots, like banks and trenches that may or may not produce the goods, depending on the species sought and the locality. But when the bottom is of a relatively uniform depth, a bait placed at 140 yd (140 m) enables him to command a zone beyond the competing baits of other anglers. Most anglers, for all their claims, can put out baits around 70 yd (70 m). This may be the edge of the runway along which the fish shoals will travel with the tide. The other side of that runway may be a mile away, or it may be as close as 180 yd (180 m). Thus the long-range bait is right in the middle, where it will attract most interest.

Some species of fish, like cod, swim close to the

UK casting champion Paul Kerry demonstrates perfect technique.

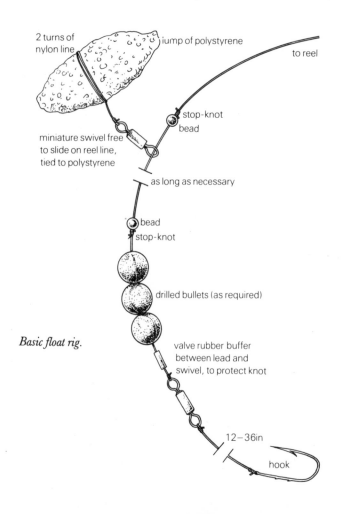

Basic float rig.

beach some days and far out at other times. Shore anglers often use two rods on specific beaches, so that they can intercept fish travelling both routes. One bait lies fairly close in, the other well out. However, if the beach is crowded, both baits are hurled out a long way. If the fish come in close, nearby short casters will catch them and the observant angler will know to adjust his tactics.

There are, of course, many times when it pays not to cast out too far. Flounders and bass, for example, often work the very edge of the tide. Obviously there is only one rule about how far to cast – only as far out as the fish are feeding.

Technique

In the overhead thump style of cast, the rod is still compressing when the sinker is let fly. In high-velocity casts, the rod is compressed totally well before this point is reached. It is probably true that most long-range casters like to feel the rod go hard, becoming fully compressed, before they give it that final clout that makes the sinker zip through the air.

With a standard pendulum cast, the sinker is swung away from the angler, parallel with the beach, then is swung back high above his head. As it is coming up, the angler positions his arms and shoulders so that he is what casters call 'under' the rod, as though the rod is to be pushed round and up in the same way that a boxer gets behind a punch. The caster then clouts the rod as hard as possible, moving it round and up, then finally he pulls in with one hand and punches with the other. Ideally this should be against a fully-compressed rod, so that the sinker accelerates just that little bit more. So where has the power come from?

At the start, most pendulum casters transfer all their weight on to the foot that is away from the sea. Some beginners have trouble with this. The best way is to bend the leg a little and position the body-weight so that perfect balance can be held on that leg. The other foot lightly touches the ground, just to add support.

At this stage, the caster's shoulders are facing away from the sea. His left arm is away from his body, with the right arm bent close towards the shoulder. At the moment of hitting the rod, power comes from the swivelling of the shoulders and trunk, the straightening of the weight-bearing leg and from the transfer of weight from that leg to the other. When these reach a climax, the arms punch and pull. At the climax the butt of the rod ends up high in the caster's chest, the up-rod arm straight, and the shoulders following through that movement. All this takes a second to execute and can only be learnt through tuition and practice.

Chapter 11
Baits

Baits can be classified as sighted, or scented, or both. To attempt to understand why a fish will take one particular bait and not another is difficult in view of the differences between the environments of fish and anglers.

Lugworm

This worm graphically betrays its presence by forming neat coils of sand on the surface of the beach. In most cases a small indenture will be found nearby. The coil and pit mark each end of the U-shaped burrow in which the lugworm spends its life. The much sought-after black, sewie, or yellow-tail lugs are generally found further down the beach, and their burrows may go down a yard or more to rich feeding strata. The more watery versions, known as the well worm, soft lug, red or blow lug, are found closer in. The bigger spring tides produce the better-quality black and leathery lugworm.

The coil-and-pit method of digging requires no more than location of the give-away marks. Digging mid-way between them will locate the worm. Better still, follow the tunnel down from the coil until the worm is located. On many beaches the former method of location does not work because there is no indent. Dig out a spit of sand from slightly ahead of the coil and then dig directly down at the rear of the spit, ensuring that you keep the burrow in view. As soon as the worm can be seen, it can be gently extracted from its tunnel. Don't pull at its soft tail as it will break off and the worm will be lost into the bowels of the sand.

There are various methods of storage, both short and long term, but the first operation is to remove the gut by gently squeezing the worm's head and drawing the finger and thumb along the body towards the head. This prevents the outer skin from becoming soft and flabby. However, if the worms are for immediate use this gutting is counter-productive as it removes a valuable source of scent.

To store lugworms for only a couple of days, either mix them in dry sand or sawdust to absorb excess moisture or wrap them individually in newspaper. Keep them in a cool place. For storage up to six months or more, the easiest method is to place a folded sheet of newspaper on the floor, lay out the worms with plenty of space in between and parallel to each other, then roll the paper into a cylinder. Place these into a polythene bag and store in the deep freeze until required.

Lugworm catches most species of fish either on its own or in a cocktail with fish or shellfish. It must stay on the hook and look like a worm, not a sloppy bundle of jelly. It is a soft bait and the operation of casting tends to tear at it, so care must be taken in threading worms up the hook and over the eye or spade-end lest you pierce the outer skin.

Ragworms

There are many species of ragworm. Most live in burrows and feed on planktonic matter extracted from the mud and water.

One species that burrows into sand or mud is the king rag, which grows to an enormous 2–3 ft (60–90 cm) long. It is tinted purple-green with a pinkish underside, but will turn an angry red and orange colour after removal from its hole. It is probably the most sought-after ragworm and the easiest to locate. Shingle beds, mussel banks and estuarine conditions are the best places to find it. It can often be located by treading around the area – water will spurt from the mouth of its tunnel. Another method, particularly on a spring tide, is to ease over some of the larger stones. Very often

Digging for lugworm, a convenience bait that is spectacularly effective at times.

the worm may be seen lying stretched along its run. Burrows are characterized by a distinctive coating of mud around them. Speed at digging is essential for this species. When they realize you have evil designs on them, they move extremely fast down into the clay or mud.

The harbour rag's name gives away its general location. It is a small worm around 3–4 in (7.5–10 cm) long, and of a brownish-green, slightly transparent hue with a blood-red line down its back. As it is more tolerant of fresh water it is found in the mud of harbours and estuaries. It lives near the surface, thus making it an easy target for the digger armed with a small garden fork, or even bare hands. A worm suited to small and fine wire hooks, it is a killer bait for flatfish, wrasse, small pollack and thin-lipped mullet.

Storage is fairly straightforward with king rag, either short or long term, but the only sure way of keeping ragworm of any species in tip-top condition is to start right at the digging stage by separating any damaged worms into a second bucket. Immediately after digging, in the case of king rag, wrap them in newspaper and inspect them each day for signs of excessive dampness, preferably changing their bed daily until all excess moisture has been absorbed. With this method the worms will stay healthy for at least a couple of weeks. The smaller versions of king rag will keep quite happily in damp, but not wet, vermiculite or sand in the salad compartment of a fridge.

Crabs

Shore crab peelers can be expected in fair quantities from about the beginning of May onwards but the full flush of peeling does not really start until June. In sun-warmed lagoons and brackish estuary drains free from the cooling tides, shore

Peeler crabs like this can charm fish from the sea when used correctly.

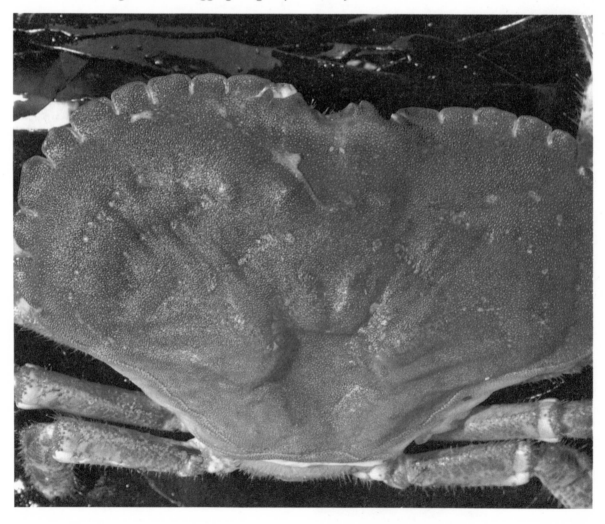

crabs can be found as early as late March, depending on the weather. Peelers are found throughout the year along the south Devon and Cornish coasts. Much depends on the severity of the preceding winter.

Take a large bucket containing weed to keep the crabs cool. Put peelers under the weed and softs on top, otherwise the peelers will cuddle the softs to pulp. Never collect more than you will require for a couple of fishing sessions.

For storage, it is imperative that they be kept in a cool environment, never in water unless aerated as they will drown through lack of oxygen. Peelers may be kept lightly chilled for up to three weeks as this lowers the body temperature, slowing down the peeling process. Softs will carry on with the hardening process until quite useless as bait and should be used up as soon as possible. Give them a reviver in sea water for a few minutes each day.

To be effective, the soft crab must be in a velvet soft condition, not partially hardened. A peeler needs to be undressed. First kill it by pressing firmly with finger and thumb between the eyes, gently lift off the back shell and peel the underside. Take off the legs and retain them, if required, for small baits. Legs and claws of large crabs like edibles can be peeled and tied into bunches. Hard leg sockets may be left on as a means of securing the hook. What remains is virtually a soft crab. Pass the hook through the body, out through a leg socket and repeat the process. Secure it with dressmaker's shirring elastic.

Crab is a natural for rock fishing, in estuaries for flounders, and on sandy beaches for bass, cod, plaice, dabs and smooth-hounds. It is widely agreed that the most effective species are velvet swimming crab, edible crab and shore crab.

Shellfish

Shellfish baits include razorfish, mussels, cockles, gaper or soft-shelled clams, butterfish, slipper limpets, piddocks and hermit crabs, which can also be included in this group. Shellfish baits come into their own after a violent storm on a beach where they live. They are also excellent stand-by baits in many situations either on their own or as cocktails with worms – mainly lug.

The razorfish is aptly named because of its shell's likeness to the old cut-throat razor. It must be the shellfish supremo. It will tempt bass, cod, rays, flatfish and many other species. It is not as easy to locate as most other shellfish, but its size

makes up for this. It is worth the trouble it takes to find.

The gaper or soft-shelled clam is a close relation to the razor and is another highly delectable bait if used in the correct circumstances. Neither is much good under a flat calm sea where the fish aren't really looking for them. But on a storm beach in the teeth of a big wind it's a different picture.

Mud flats and estuaries are the haunts of this species which is spoon-shaped and grows to about 5 in (12.5 cm) long. Unlike the firm flesh of the razor, the clam has a soft body which does not stay well on the hook. It is safer to discard the body and be content with the syphon or shoe. This is covered by a thin brown skin which needs to be removed to reveal firm white flesh.

The mussel is a good stand-by bait, easily collected and stored in tanks, and is often a good tempter for shy-feeding fish when worms aren't effective. Mussel is a very soft bait and many shore anglers steer well clear of it because of its poor casting qualities. It is ideal for rocky ledge situations where casting isn't necessary, or for float fishing. Codling, pollack, coalfish, plaice and wrasse often go silly after mussel bait, so here is a method of hardening it for the hook.

First it has to be parted from its shell. Hone down the business end of a teaspoon so that the front edge is quite sharp. The end of the handle is also reduced in thickness to be used as a lever when prising open the shell. The spoon is used to scoop the meat and muscle cleanly away from the shell.

The mussels are then placed in a sieve above a bowl and liberally sprinkled with household salt. After two or three hours in a cool place the salt will have drawn out the excess moisture, thus tightening up the meat and producing a firmer bait. Wrap them in newspaper to keep them firm. A couple of turns of shirring elastic will complete the exercise. A system of making cocktails, where hard casting is vital to success, is to thread mussels on to the hook, lay black lug alongside and tie them with thread to the mussels like splints. The same method of preparation also applies to some of the smaller species of shellfish such as slipper limpets, scallops and carpet shells.

Fish baits

Into this category we can place such species as sand-eels, sprats, mackerel, herring, and squid which, although a mollusc, is nevertheless a fishy type of bait. Although fish baits are generally stand-bys, many species are partial to them. The oily species are the most highly scented. Their attractiveness lies in the combination of sight and scent. A strip of mackerel is a deadly spinning bait and equally good fished statically.

A live sand-eel, lightly hooked through the top of its back, can be an absolute killer when free-lined from a rock ledge or jetty for bass, pollack and other mid-water predators. A baiting needle is a handy tool for threading the line through the mouth and down the spine before tying on the hook, which should be secured to the tail with either cotton or shirring elastic. Don't mutilate the little fish or cut it into bits because it must look realistic to be of any effect.

Whitebait may be used in a manner similar to sand-eels (and elvers, when hooked behind the head to prevent them squirming around the trace). These can very often be collected in their hundreds from the shoreline after mackerel have trapped a shoal and forced it up on to the beach.

The faithful old mackerel proves excellent at times. It must be frozen very fresh to last any length of time. It is an excellent stand-by species if you are a little hard up for baits, and has a place all of its own when fishing for congers, silver eels, bull huss, doggies and other species.

Presentation is governed by which species you intend to fish for. Fishing for whiting or pollack with a chunk cut indiscriminately might attract a bite but may not hook the fish. But cut a neat thin lask from the tail and tidily pass the hook through a couple of times and you will likewise attract the same bite and succeed in hooking the fish. The relationship of bait size to species hunted gains greater importance with fish baits. Tail sections or whole fish when used for tope, conger, rays or bass must be secured so as to allow the hook to face outwards, otherwise many fish will be missed due to the hook being struck back into the meat and not into the fish. The needle is again useful for threading line through the bait.

Herrings are generally shop-bought and therefore slightly stale in even the best circumstances, so examine them well prior to purchase. Your best bet is to buy direct from the boats that catch them. They freeze well and can be used like mackerel. Sprats, when dead, appeal mainly to scavenging fish but rarely predators, which have little difficulty in catching these slow-moving fish on the fin.

Squid is used for species under circumstances similar to those where mackerel or herring are used. One form is the smaller Californian Kalamari, which measures 4–6 in (10–15 cm) long, and makes an ideal hook-size bait. Another is the larger European species, best bought from the dockside, which may be sliced up or used as larger static baits or in boot-lace strips for spinning and float fishing. The freezer is the best storage system. Buy a large box and partially thaw its occupants for repacketing.

The Kalamari must be presented as naturally as possible for maximum effect, in order that it may double as a sighted and scented bait. Pass the hook through the body and through the head between the eyes before tying on with elastic thread at the head. The hook must stand proud else it may be choked on the strike through the flesh catching on predatory teeth.

Shrimps and prawns

These easily-collected baits are particularly effective in clear water from rocks, piers or jetties. Shrimps can be amassed with a suitable net pushed along the low-water line of sandy shores. Select the larger ones and place them in a bucket of sea water which is aerated by a portable pump. Alternatively, change the water constantly. Live shrimps are far superior to dead ones.

Fished live these crustaceans are superb fish catchers, producing viscious bites from pollack and bass. Pouting bite the tails off. To present them alive, insert the hook point into a small V-shaped indentation among the legs close to the head. This avoids the vital area – the dark spot inside the body. They may also be hooked through the third or fourth body segment. For pier, drift and floatfishing, the head method appears more natural because the hook lies underneath. Small-ish, fine-wire hooks are light enough to allow them to stay active for some time. The aquarium is ideal for long-term storage.

Lures

These are sighted baits (not forgetting vibrations, of course), which attract by colour, shape and movement. Lures are designed in a vast variety of shapes, colours and sizes, and care must be taken to place these items into perspective as to their possible effectiveness. The basic lures used in shore fishing are spoons, spinners, feathers and soft plastic sand-eels.

Selecting a useful spoon is not difficult.

Remember that the difference between two spoons of equal weight, but of different size, is that the one with the smaller blade area will sink faster, work deeper, and cast easier against the wind. The spoon with the greater surface area will sink more slowly and swim higher in the water. A spoon is designed to wobble and flutter. You will have to judge the depth of water and correct speed of retrieval so that the lure is wobbling at fish level.

There are times when a spinner will catch fish where a spoon will not – and vice versa. In some respects a spinner is more versatile because it can be relied on to fish more slowly as the blade offers more resistance to the water. So it can be used without snagging in knee-deep situations. The trick when using a spinner is to estimate where the fish are shoaling and then over-cast and bring the lure back to them. Don't forget that fish sense vibrations long before they sight a bait or lure. Movement is of more interest to the predator at the first moment of contact than the colour, shape or size.

Whilst the original coloured, feathered lures are still effective at catching fish, there are now on the market many variations on the theme which far outfish the feather. A range of fluorescent plastic tube and feather, silver ribbon, or sparkling mylar tinsel outfits have taken over as representations of shoals of fry.

Plastic and rubber eels are proven fish catchers. Fish the smaller sizes in tandem on short snoods, or the larger ones on flowing-trace type rigs, which may be weighted above for casting. Or use a long-trace paternoster. A trolling situation from rock marks or jetties allows natural movement of this type of lure, which often works well when held steady in a current, with periodic upward sweeps of the rod to make it spurt forwards, then fall back. Colour is frequently most important.

For casting rubber eels on light line, weight them with split shot inside the body cavity. This may improve the motion through the water. There are other types of soft plastic fish with superb tail vibrations which are well worth testing.

Nothing to get nervous about. Tope tails provide a firm grip which prevents the fish from biting your legs.

Chapter 12
Predators, cod and bass

Predators

Tope

Under the right circumstances, tope are undoubtedly the most glamorous and exciting fish for the shore angler to latch into. They are found all round the British Isles, though the best shore fishing is probably along the Western fringe, with south-west Ireland offering excellent opportunities.

Tackle need be no more powerful than is necessary to hurl a bait out there. If you can achieve this objective with a bass rod casting 2–3 oz (60–90 g) sinkers, then the ensuing battle will be great fun. Plenty of line is needed, at least 250 yd (250 m) in most places and maybe 400 yd (400 m) on very shallow beaches.

At the business end a special running paternoster is employed. A 4/0–6/0 hook, honed to a needle-sharp point, is crimped to one end of 2 ft (60 cm) of braided trace wire. You can use 200 lb (90 kg) wire if it is supple. Thickish wire doesn't deter tope, and it takes the crimps better than fine wire, which tope have been known to bite through. At the other end is a reasonably large swivel. The other end of the swivel is knotted to a rubbing leader of around 80 lb (36 kg) test. This not only takes the shock of the cast, but also the rubbing of the rough skin of a hooked tope which would otherwise cut the line. Immediately above this swivel should be slid a large bead to prevent a split-ring jambing over the swivel. This ring needs to be large enough to slide over the leader-knot unchecked when a fish makes off with the bait. About 3 ft (90 cm) of standard leader line connect this ring to a sinker, above which a bait clip will facilitate casting. This clip should be larger than usual to prevent the bulky bait from flying free in mid-cast.

When a tope takes, it sets the reel screeching. No! Don't panic! With the reel in free spool and the check on, a bite is signified by a couple of bobs at the rod tip before it bends down as the fish sets off on a ridiculously unnecessary sprint. Let the fish take line – as much as it wants – without feeling any drag at all. It will eventually slow down, turn the bait and start gulping it back as it moves off again more slowly. Wind down hard and run backwards, bumping the hook home as you go. Keep the drag at a safe setting, applying additional pressure with a thumb, for when a fish takes off in panic, too tight a drag will pop the line. Normally the fish will run up and down the shoreline, not out to sea. If it is held too hard it will try to roll up the leader and may touch the line with its rough body.

Play the fish out, get the leader back on to the reel and walk the fish out through the surf and tail it. Hold it by the tail and dorsal or pectoral fin to prevent rupture of the internal organs. Slosh the head back and forth in the water so as to pass water over the gills of the exhausted fish to revive it. Rock anglers should take an efficient pair of snips rather than a gaff with them. Make the wire trace into a loop, passed once through the eye of the hook and held closed right there with a few turns of thread. To release the fish, snip through one side and the fish will be released as the wire slides out through the eye of the hook.

Tope baits should be as fresh and bloody as possible. Mackerel, herring and other oily fish are ideal. Squid also works, as do chunks of silver eel and small mullet – conservation permitting. Tope will eat soft crab, and they'll occasionally take baits intended for lesser fry. Greater sand-eels catch well in some places, and frozen trout are increasing in popularity. Whatever bait you use, it must be well mounted and changed as soon as the scent washes out.

Dogfish

Among this gang of little sharks are the lesser-spotted dog fish, the greater-spotted dog (also called bull huss), the black-mouthed dogfish (a deep-water species from the north), the spurdog, and the two smooth-hounds. Some anglers have difficulty differentiating between the species. The black-mouthed species has a black mouth. The lesser-spotted dog has little spots and, sometimes, a pouting-like banded appearance. The greater-spotted dog has more blotchy spots and its nasal flaps are separate while those of the lesser-spotted are joined. Big bull huss are reckoned by some to be worth catching. Small ones are insignificant enough to make it of little importance whether or not you can tell them apart from lesser-spotteds.

The starry smooth-hound has light-coloured spots along its upper half and a fairly smooth skin while the other one has a rough skin and no spots. Their teeth are flat grinders like those of most rays. This is where they differ from tope, which have fearful dentition. Spur-dogs have disconcerting green eyes and wickedly sharp spurs ahead of each dorsal fin.

Fish legered baits on the sea-bed for best results. A 40 lb (18 kg) nylon hook-link defeats their teeth. Apart from their eating qualities, there's not much good to be said for them.

The smooth-hounds, however, are a different kettle of dogfish. Indeed, it is unfortunate that they are not found in greater numbers. These two species are very fond of crustaceans, which may explain why they're uncommon outside estuarine waters like the Thames, the Solent and the Bristol Channel. Where they can be caught from the shore they offer great sport. For a species that spends its normal day chugging about the sea-bed in search of crabs, whelks and similar fare, these species have an amazing turn of speed and frequently leap when hooked. This makes them the odd-balls of the dogfish camp.

The wise angler arms himself with the lightest outfit possible, terminating in a standard running leger or whatever he fancies, and baits with peeler crab for preference, baby squid, squid strip or ragworm. A rubbing leader is advised – 40 lb (18 kg) nylon – when using light line for hounds.

High summer is their season, going into autumn when the bigger fish show up. Runs of these species vary in strength from year to year, but as little is known about their biology and seasonal movements, no explanation can be offered for this phenomenon. Both prefer the warm, settled conditions that favour tope fishing.

Rays

May through to July are the best months for shore rays, though odd ones – especially small-eyeds – are taken right through to November if the weather holds. The average shore thornback is 5–8 lb (2.25–3.50 kg) or better where commercial pressure is light enough to allow a degree of longevity. Their maximum weight is 40 lb (18 kg). In winter they move off to more equable temperatures offshore.

Preferred habitats for thornbacks are shallow depressions among sand, mud, gravel, shell grit and so on out of the current, where there is a moderate depth of water. They are more widely dispersed when there is little strength in the tide. Estuaries and sea lochs are favourite places, and sandy patches among reefs. They are also fond of the shallow gulleys that run along some sandy beaches. They appear to realize that they are not too agile, and they don't take the risk of being stranded by the tide through coming too close to the edge. Long casting is often vital for success. Thornbacks tend to move down the tide. If after a succession of bites there comes a quiet spell, a move along the beach could put you back among the flock.

A standard 5–6 oz (150–180 g) rod is perfect for rays. Heavy leads carry big baits out to the ravening hordes more effectively than lighter sinkers. A bass rod is sufficiently potent to play most rays. However, the ability to place a bait well out from the shore is frequently the one factor that produces fish. Adequate end-tackle is a running paternoster, with a casting leader and a 40 lb (18 kg) hook line to cope not only with the ray's crushing teeth but with sharp spines that frequently tangle and chafe the tackle. Best results inshore come to baits with scent-appeal anchored to the sea-bed. These should be mounted on strong 4/0–6/0 hooks like the O'Shaughnessy or the Sundridge Specimen Longshank which will withstand a good chew.

Baits include peeler crab, hermit crabs, fresh-minted herrings, sprats and mackerel – or chunks thereof with the hook passed around the backbone for firm anchorage – king ragworm, bunches of lugworm, baby squids, squid strips, sand-eels, fresh pouting and sometimes razorfish. All baits should ooze juices and scent. Rays have good noses but poor vision, so baits should be changed when the attractiveness washes out. A groundbait trail will bring rays from afar. The rod tip will

Thornback rays – just one of several ray species available from British beaches.

bounce, tremble and buck a few times when a ray bites; the line may even slacken off. Do nothing until the fish moves off. Too great a hurry foul-hooks the fish or pulls the bait away. The hook needs to be well inside the mouth in order to obtain a good hold. Point the rod along the line, wind up the slack, then belt the point home. Rays fight by deflecting water off their backs so that they can adhere to the sea-bed.

Gaff in a wing, if necessary, though a net is a more refined piece of equipment. To remove the hook, flip the fish on to its back. It is kindest to make an incision along the barb to remove the hook; this is preferable to a wrestling match, which would damage fish intended for return. But take care – jaws that crush crabs can do the same to fingers.

Small-eyed rays are caught mainly from deep-water beaches and sand patches at the base of rocky outcrops from the Isle of Wight westwards to Wales and the south and west of Ireland. Their season corresponds with that of the thornback, with an average size of 5lb (2.25kg). Similar habitat and habits obtain for both species, except that small-eyeds don't move as far up estuaries. The killer bait for this species is sand-eel, especially fast-frozen ones, which often outfish fresh. Its distinguishing pattern is of white lines that run parallel with the edges of the wings, a white fringe to the disc, and light-coloured (and some dark-coloured) spots on a greyish background.

Sting-rays

Late April, if the inshore shallows have been dosed with sunshine, is the earliest one can take sting-rays from the shore, with the summer months offering best sport. Hot, calm weather is best. The trouble with such weather is that the shore crabs hold a ceaseless fiesta and ravenously guzzle baits as fast as the angler can get them out there.

Standard shore-casting rods are adequate. The reel's drag must be smooth enough to cope with a battling stinger. Line of around 0.40mm is ideal. Hook links of 30lb (14kg) nylon will withstand their grinding teeth. Any bottom-fishing end-tackle will suffice. Baits should be king rag, peeler crab or lugworm for preference – depending on locality – and sometimes mollusc, fish or squid baits appeal.

In shallow water, the usual reaction to the angler setting the hook into a big stinger is a small eruption on the surface. Land the fish either by towing it ashore with the leader, or using a net. A small gaff can be slipped into the leading edge of a wing, but as stingers are inedible, a gaff should not really be used because an infection may set into the wound. A landing net not only restrains a lashing tail but also allows the angler to tip the fish back into the water with minimal distress.

Conger.

Conger eels

Summer and autumn are the best times to fish inshore for congers. For most of the summer they hole up in lairs, but as autumn approaches many migrate along the coast, often tracking the shoals of midget pouting and whiting, well away from dense cover. In shallow littoral waters they migrate out deeper as the year cools down, but in a mild winter plenty stay close to shore in moderately deep water and may be caught out – sometimes fatally – by a sudden cold spell. In the West Country, and where the North Atlantic Drift provides a warming influence, congers can be caught from the shore throughout a warm winter.

While standard beach-casting tackle is adequate where congers can be taken in snagless areas, a 30 lb (14 kg) class boat rod, multiplier reel and 30 lb (14 kg) line will prove most useful from piers and harbour walls – the best fishing area there is close in to the structure, so casting isn't necessary. The fighting of a conger involves levering it up in the water, so too long a rod permits the conger to apply excessive leverage against the angler. When fishing from rocks, a 9–10 ft (2.74–3.00 m) weapon is advisable. Casting distance should be minimal because the further the fish is away from the angler, the greater its chances of hanging on to a rock with its tail as it is being brought ashore. Under such circumstances, it is best to lob out a short way so that much of the fight involves lifting the conger away from the rough stuff rather than pulling it over the top. So the shortish rod should have plenty of meat in its middle to allow the angler to use it as a lever.

Braided wire isn't necessary for conger traces. A 2 ft (60 cm) length of 100–150 lb (45–70 kg) commercial nylon, carefully crimped to a hook and a good swivel, will defeat their teeth. Traces of stiff stainless steel wire are sold in some shops.

Big baits are used for conger, so hooks of 6/0 to 10/0 are ideal. They should be strong – O'Shaughnessy type are perfect – and of carbon steel rather than stainless as nylon traces can be cut close to the hook for returning unwanted fish. The hook will rust out without harming the fish. End the trace with a clip so that congers can be dealt with at leisure – sometimes the feeding spell may be very brief. Take plenty of spare traces – and test each one after making it, to check for flaws in the crimping of the heavy nylon. If it is crimped too hard, the nylon may be damaged. Never be tempted to retrieve a trace from a conger until it is well dead.

Congers feed best during dull conditions by day, except when out and about in the autumn after small whiting. In harbours where fish are gutted or lobster pots baited, they'll feed by day if there hasn't been any activity for several days and therefore no free food. From rocks, which offer low light values, congering can be good by day, and where there is a fair depth of water. But night-time is best of all. They aren't too fond of rough seas and strong currents, though they'll feed when surf is rushing over shallow reef. Flat calms, with a hint of sea fog or thunder have always given me best sport, especially during a slow, ebb tide. After dark, congers leave their lairs to feed. They can be caught in deep gullies like the ones bass anglers leap over to reach other parts of a reef. As a general rule, flying-ant weather is ideal.

Baits should be fresh. Only ravenous fish will take stale baits. Groundbait, as used for tope, will bring the fish around. Baits include live and dead fish like pouting, whiting, herrings, mackerel, small pollack, wrasse and so on. Squid and cuttlefish are excellent, if very fresh. Congers are most partial to a large edible peeler crab. They'll take lugworm at times – and even fillets of conger if hungry enough. Harbour congers may become accustomed to scavenging, though there are few harbours nowadays where fish waste is dumped overboard. Hook all fish baits through the head, using a large hook and passing it through the eye sockets. Congers always take baits from the head.

Don't be in a hurry to strike. Wait until the fish has moved off with the bait, then thump home the hook. Strike too soon and the conger will hang on to the bait for a while, then spit it out. When fishing into rocks and other snags, wind the conger up off the bottom for as far as possible before banging home the hook. It often surprises people how willingly they will allow themselves to be led. The strike is generally met with a series of shoulder-wrenching jolts. For this reason, many anglers use a boat angler's belly pad to cushion the stomach from bruising.

You can't often catch and gaff a conger on your own. Most times a friend is required to wield the gaff – or a knife lashed to a pole to cut the trace and release the fish. The secret of landing a conger in the dark is to be totally prepared and not to hurry. The gaff-man won't be thankful if he has to land a fish that is still full of fight. Once you can hold it away from danger, fight it out, if possible, in open water. Don't use brute force, but skill, and retain the initiative!

Eighty-three and still fishing, but fish stocks have declined a great deal in his lifetime.

A strong gaff is vital. One with an unscrewable head should have this locked in the handle with a split pin. Or use a pukka gaff. Congers writhe and try to twist off, so only a strong gaff will do. Little ones will end up bent and useless. An alternative is to use a flying gaff with a removable handle, the head fixed to a rope.

Once a conger's head is turned for home, keep her coming. If she wants to dive, let her go at the last second so she doesn't break the line. Expert judgement is needed here and the ability to feel how much pressure the fish is putting on to the line. Some are lost when they regain a sanctuary and get their tails round a rock. Sometimes they'll be bluffed into letting go if you slacken off and leave them in peace for a couple of minutes. Most times, however, this allows them to reach an even better sanctuary.

When the man comes to gaff it, keep the line tight else the spinning eel will wind line round its body. The gaff is best lodged either just behind the head or near the vent, with the former position best.

Don't stab at a live conger's head with a knife. If the eel twists while you're doing this you stand a good chance of having your hand severely gashed by the knife. Instead, drag the fish on the gaff – and the bigger the gaff, the less able it will be to writhe off it – to a safe place, then thwack her across the back close to the vent with a lump of wood. This is where the lymph heart is, and the fish will then be quietened. Now a knife can be banged through the spine just behind the head, if you feel the need.

Mackerel

Early in the year, inshore mackerel feed extensively on plankton, which they sieve through their gill rakers. The resultant sludge, varying from orange to dark green, depending on the plankton species, may account for the old wife's tale that this species eats sewage. Or it may be because mackerel often herd fry into a current that flows around the end of a sewer. From rock marks it is common to see mackerel swimming slowly along with their nose clear of the water, their mouth open as they strain out the food.

They largely ignore spinners while doing this and will dive in unison when one lands too close. These fish will sometimes take very small lures, but foul-hooking is more likely. When feeding on small fry, mackerel rush through them, again with their mouths open, straining fish from the water. Small fish – and angler's lures – are attacked individually.

Fry swim close to the surface, feeding on plankton, moving against wind-induced surface drift. So a northerly wind brings them close in to south coast beaches. Estuaries suck fry into them when the tide is making. The mackerel follow. Other feeding areas are rocky headlands, tide races and overfalls, and corners between the beach and a harbour wall. They feed by herding the fry into the current or trapping them against the surface or in a tight corner. Mackerel attacks are less haphazard than many would imagine.

Mackerel are mainly sight feeders, and are caught most easily when the water is clear. They dislike heavy seas and chilly weather, when they move out from the shoreline to deeper water. Early morning and late evening are the best times to catch them. Rarely do they move into very shallow water or work along the beach at low tide, but come closest at high water. This is less critical when fishing from rocks and piers.

When after mackerel for bait, use a string of three or four feathers tied on size 1 stainless steel

Garfish.

O'Shaughnessy hooks. Instead of a lead weight at the end, use a small pirk which will cause the feathers to move more erratically through the water and send out come-hither flashes. For this reason, when one fish strikes, leave it out there. Its flashing gyrations make the others believe it has found a large shoal of fry and they'll come looking. Use a bass rod, reel and light line for this. If the fish are well out, heavier casting tackle will be necessary.

Most times the fish will be close to the surface, so the lighter the end tackle, the more slowly and seductively it can be retrieved. A heavy sinker often causes the feathers to fish below the feeding zone. Watch other anglers, noting the weights they use and the speed of retrieval. Results that come to a heavy sinker fished slowly should be interpreted as a sign that the fish are feeding close to the sea-bed.

When they're right on top, thumb the spool and start to wind when the tackle is some 10 ft (3 m) from hitting water. Thus the gear will fish at the surface. Don't cast into the middle of travelling mackerel shoals, but a few yards ahead, giving them a shot-gunner's lead, else the tackle may land astern of the shoal and be ignored. Many anglers use a violent sink-and-draw motion when feathering. This is counter-productive. A steady retrieve catches more fish while a jerky motion snatches the lures away from attacking fish.

Self-weighted spinners weighing $\frac{5}{8}$–1 oz (15–30 g), feathered lures fished paternoster style, a single feather with a couple of swan-shots crimped close to the hook – all of these provide excellent sport when fished on a light spinning outfit.

Garfish

Gars arrive a little before mackerel, between April and May, depending on locality.

The gar's beak shows that it feeds mainly by seizing fry. It is more astute than mackerel. Sometimes it is caught on spinners, but these must be small or slender and fitted with small hooks. Rarely do gars take feathers. The best method is float-fished mackerel skin. Tiny jigs can be made from size 6 hooks dressed with white chicken feathers. One or two swan-shots are crimped to the line just ahead of the eye. A very light rod, fine line and a small fixed-spool reel are best for casting these out to where the shoals of garfish can be seen swirling at the surface. Sometimes they leap while feeding.

Because of the beak, gars have problems hitting spinners. They use it as a truncheon, sometimes tapping a lure several times before the hook bites them. Float-fished skin baits are easier for them to take. Even so, the float is likely to bob several times before the fish moves off.

Pollack

Clear Atlantic water is the best place to hunt for decent-size pollack. They prefer deepish water. Schools of immature fish abound around piers along the south-eastern shores of England, while the West Country, South Wales, south and west Ireland, the west of Scotland and the outer isles that benefit from the North Atlantic Drift current all produce good specimens. Pollack thin out in colder northern waters where coalfish take over (as in Yorkshire, North Wales and the eastern coast of Scotland; both species are fairly abundant on the west coast).

Pollack free the angler from the necessity of collecting bait. Feathered lures, spinners and red-gill sand-eels all work well. Red eels are a proven killer bait for pollack. Weighted lures can be tied direct to the reel line while those without weight (often more effective because of this) should be fished on a long-trace paternoster.

Depending on locality and the size of the fish present, tackle need be no more powerful than a flimsy spinning rod and a small fixed-spool loaded with fine line, on up to a light beach-caster and a multiplier loaded with heavier string. Such an outfit would be used where heavy fish are found among tangled weeds and giant boulders. In this respect, it is worth tying on a 1–2 oz (30–60 g) sinker and using it as a long-range plummet to explore a strange, deep-water mark. Count it down between the time it hits surface and reaches the sea-bed. Retrieve it slowly along the sea-bed. Thus a picture can be constructed of the underwater topography before any expensive spinners become snagged up.

Early in the year, pollack will travel into estuaries and pick off salmon and seatrout smolts migrating down to the sea. Big fish that turn up unexpectedly in autumn and winter are believed to be from those groups that tag along behind migrating shoals of herrings and sprats.

If a bait is fished too high above their ambush, pollack will ignore it. This is why best results come to those who live dangerously, fishing close to the kelp. As dusk approaches, the fish move close to the surface, sometimes even jumping out as they

Pollack country.

hit a surface-fished lure. When a big pollack hits close to the surface, it dives for the bottom again with the throttle wide. The reel's drag must be set at around half the breaking strain of the line in order to control the dive. Extra pressure can be applied with a thumb or finger to the spool. Pollack are good at popping lines, so don't tighten the drag too far and never try to stop a pollack dead in its tracks when diving at full power.

Under bright daylight conditions, catches are often only of small fish. Some days it is possible to see the golden flashes as pollack come to a lure, refuse it, then dive back to the sea-bed. Evening and early morning are the best times of day. When they are close to the surface, excellent sport can be had even with small specimens on fly tackle designed for reservoir trout fishing. A slow-sinking shooting-head and streamer lures are ideal.

By autumn, pollack shoals have become markedly nomadic. Very big fish track the concentrations of herrings and sprats. Some of these specimens roam close inshore and provide a pleasant surprise in autumn and early winter. The equinoctial gales generally disperse pollack from

Terry Carroll casts with his reel low down the butt, even though this increases leverage against him from big fish.

the inshore reefs, although Indian summers are known to produce superb sport, even up to November, with small-medium specimens. As the year draws to its close, the fish move off to deep-water reefs and wrecks in preparation for spring spawning.

Cod

Tackle

A good cod rod must be powerful enough to project a 6oz (1.80g) weight complete with bait to distances of 150yd (150m) if required. It must have sufficient tip flexibility to receive bites from that distance and be pokey enough to deal effectively with a large, powerful fish in heavy seas. Sensitivity must be sacrificed when removing cod from their natural habitat and a potent weapon is required to overcome both fish and environment. Monofil line of 15–20lb (6.75–9kg) will suffice on most sand and shingle beaches, but once over rock 30–40lb (14–18kg) line may be necessary just to have a fighting chance against the terrain. Some Yorkshire anglers go as high as 70lb (32kg) test.

To combat the tremendous strain imposed by long-distance casting, a shock leader is required. When complete with bait, the terminal rig must be sufficiently streamlined to permit long casting and allow the bait to stay firmly in one spot. On many occasions, the sea will be full of loose weed and simplicity of tackle helps keep the angler's sanity on an even keel. It is for these reasons that the ubiquitous paternoster comes up trumps.

Once baited, the hook length is held close to the main leader by means of a bait clip. When codding with lugworm, it is wise to fix a coarse angler's leger stop a few inches away from the hook to prevent the worms sliding up the trace.

In early autumn, when the sea is swarming with whiting, pouting, dabs and small codling a two- or three-hook paternoster will produce a good mixed bag. Because the hooks are smaller than those used when the bigger fish are about, and the baits correspondingly smaller, bait clips aren't required. When the big mommas hit the shoreline, a single hook paternoster will produce the goods. When they are about, it is much wiser to load one hook with plenty of bait than to divide it between three smaller hooks.

Early in the season, Mustad Aberdeens and Breakaway Spearpoints will suffice for the general mixed fishing. Both makes are lethal and ensure that any mischievous codling attempting to play kiss-chase with the bait gets its just deserts. By November, when the plump ladies are around, use a medium-gauge 4/0 or 5/0 carefully sharpened to give it a better chance of snagging into that fleshy mineshaft of a mouth. Don't be shy of using a decent size hook.

Another ace up the sleeve of the successful shore cod fisherman is the two-hook tandem live-bait rig. Sometimes conventional baits just don't score either because they aren't large enough or because the big specimens become preoccupied with chomping pouting and whiting. Double-figure cod are lazy fish and require a lot of food. Faced with the prospect of spending hours foraging for lugworm or alternatively eating two small whiting, they invariably plump for the latter.

The rig is made by tying a length of 30 lb (14 kg) line to the bottom of the shank of a well-honed 5/0

Three good cod are the prize for a successful night's fishing.

with a spade-end knot. A size 1–1/0 is fixed 3–4 in (7.5–10 cm) away from this.

Steep shingle beaches

Long casting with fresh black lug is a deadly combination for cod from steep beaches. When a winter's gale has been raging from the south-west for a few days and suddenly the barometer rises with the wind turning to the north-east and then dropping, ideal conditions occur. Shellfish, lugworm and every conceivable marine knick-knack will have been wrenched from the sea-bed and will be washing ashore.

When these excellent fishing conditions prevail it matters not one jot whether you fish the day or night tides. The sea is a murky brown colour and the fish are just too pre-occupied with food to care. The tide has just begun to flood so there is no hurry. Tackle up and clip on a 6 oz (180 g) grapnel weight. Spend a few minutes warming up with progressively longer casts. Besides, dry line is very

prone to tangling. Once confidence has built up, put some real power into those casts.

Now bait the hook with two glistening black lug and maybe a razorfish washed up at your feet. Before casting, walk 30–60 yd (30–60 m) up-tide from your position depending on the strength of tide, and then let fly. Once the tackle hits water, thumb the spool to a halt, then let the tide take enough slack line to form a belly as you walk back to your peg. After a few minutes it will tighten up and half a dozen turns of the handle will pull the rod tip hard over to the line running straight out in front of you. When a strong sea is running with a big tide – and maybe wind behind both – merely casting out and tightening the line immediately will not allow the essential bow to form up-tide from your stance, so the grip-wires won't have a chance to bite into the sea-bed.

Bites from small fish are signified by a gentle nodded greeting. Big fish tap once or twice, then accelerate away. Other times, the cod will charge the bait and the tip will spring straight as the fish pulls the wires clear of the sea-bed and carries on shorewards. Sometimes it is wise to strike these bites. Most often the jolt of the fish coming up hard against the anchored weight will snub the hook home. Only strike once, either by running back up the beach or by winding down before belting the hook home. Repeated savage striking will tear a hole in the fish's mouth.

Slowly pump the fish ashore, using the waves. Take your time and don't panic. Once the cod is in the surf, back off the reel clutch a little because if a swell takes it at this stage the hook could tear free or the line snap.

Shallow-water beaches
The cod caught along these beaches are generally of a lower average size, but present in large numbers. Double-figure fish are rarer. Aim to place the bait into the slightly deeper water in front of or behind the sandbanks that characterize these beaches because the fish invariably feed along the troughs. Look also for fish-attracting gullies and cross-tide obstructions behind which fish may shelter. Tackle and techniques are similar to those used for deep-water codding except that 5 oz (150 g) breakaway leads are normally adequate with reel lines of 12–15 lb (5.50–6.75 kg).

Pier fishing
Every pier seems to have its special cod corners and these positions are eagerly contested. Don't

employ potentially lethal casting styles; distance is unimportant. A 90 yd (90 m) lob is usually adequate. By increasing the length of your shock leader to 15 yd (15 m) you can lift codling up to 5 lb (2.25 kg) slowly by hand up the side of the pier.

Rods should never be left unattended. When a big tide is running a cod merely has to exert a few pounds of extra pressure to catapult your outfit over the side. So tie an unattended rod to the pier rail with a rod bag.

Rock fishing, Yorkshire style
The traditional method is to employ a stout glass rod with a large Scarborough centre-pin winch, loaded with 55–70 lb (25–30 kg) line. The terminal rig is a simple paternoster with a 4 ft (1.2 m) lead link and 1 ft (30 cm) hook link, both of weaker line, coming off a large swivel. Expendable weights of about 6 oz (180 g) are used.

Peeler crab and lugworm/mussel cocktails prove effective. Invest in a good pair of studded boots – not waders and fish with a companion. Always pay attention to both tidal and weather conditions.

When rock fishing in other areas, sinkers can be lost thus: form the end of the leader into a loop and tie a few inches of 6 lb (2.70 kg) line from the loop to the eye of the lead or whatever. Take a panel pin 1½ in (3.8 cm) long and impale on it a wee piece of expanded polystyrene. Poke the leader loop through the sinker eye, insert the pin and cast. When the tackle hits the sea-bed, the pin will float free and allow the angler to retain tension to his weight through very light line.

Bass

Surf fishing
March is the earliest one can open a bass season. In England, the first of the schoolies are caught from western estuaries by anglers fishing for flounders. These little fish are best ignored. The best March sport comes from Irish Atlantic storm beaches like those along Brandon Bay and at Inch in County Kerry. Tackle need be no more powerful than a standard 11–12 ft (3.35–3.65 m) fast-action bass rod, casting up to 3 oz (90 g) sinkers. Sometimes a light cod rod is required with 3–4 oz (90–120 g) leads in really wild surfs. But if such tackle is needed, the bass are unlikely to be around in force. Tumultuous surfs rarely produce good catches, but they may yield the odd monster fish. Find a sheltered corner, however, and the bass

could be concentrated there.

The type of water to look for is a surf with a steady pattern of heavy breakers. Such a surf is likely to have been born way out in the ocean. At other times, a rising sea after a period of calm or a decreasing surf after a big storm can prove rewarding. Generally the bass will be inshore of the breaking waves and in the water tables, the spent waves rushing towards the sand. The tables push ahead of them small flatfish, shrimps, swimming crabs and similar food, while the back-draw of the water carries this food seawards. Thus a band of food is created 60–120 yd (60–120 m) out, and the bass will be there. In very heavy surf, the fish will be outside the breakers, while in weak surf they'll be scattered over a wide band.

Clip a light reel to your rod, load it with 10 lb (4.50 kg) line, tie on a 25 lb (11.5 kg) casting leader and finish off with a standard paternoster. Long traces just get tangled. Bait the 2/0 hooks with rag, lug, squid strip, live or dead sand-eel. Chest waders are helpful here, but as they're expensive you may prefer to improvise with ordinary waders and over-trousers and keep the trouser ends closed tight to the boots with elastic bands or waterproof tape. Thus surging surf is prevented from filling your boots, even when a wave slops right up to your waist. Stand in the water rather than paddling at the edge – too much line out spoils bite detection. Remember that the back-draw of the water is sucking sand from under your feet. Every now and then you'll have to step out of a small pit.

After casting out your 2–4 oz (60–120 g) breakaway lead, wind in the slack line and note the angle it enters the surf. If a side-wind has caused it to belly to one side, walk along until your line enters the water at right angles to the surf. Thus the waves will run up the line rather than rolling it ahead of them. Bite detection will be easier. Bites vary from gentle tugs to full-blooded pulls and slack-liners. In all cases either run backwards to make the contact and set the hook, or wind until the fish is felt then bump the hook home. Instant action is required or the fish might

With perfect weather, tide, sea conditions, time of day, bait and tackle, this bassman cannot fail to score. He later landed a seven pounder.

move on. For the beginner, some experience will be needed to sort out bites from the sudden lifting of the sinker by a big wave and the plucks of the surf.

Playing the fish is easy enough provided you remember to fight the fish and not the surf. By reeling in and trotting backwards, or letting the fish take line when the back-draw takes it, you can use the surf to your advantage and beach the fish.

Surf beaches may look somewhat featureless. It often pays to fish near any feature – be it a small stream entering the surf, or a lump of rock, or maybe you know where a tidal current licks the shore. The edges of surf beaches, among rocky, rubbly reef, often produce more fish than at the centre.

Because most surf fishing is practised on beaches that strip a long way with the tide, take a couple of spare leads, leader and trace line, hooks, elastic thread and other vital items out there in your pockets. A polythene bag in another pocket filled with enough bait for a few hours will obviate the long trudge back to the high water line and also rules out the necessity of moving tackle bags

back with the tide. A rod rest is a nuisance and landing nets and gaffs are quite unnecessary.

Rock bass
Standard rock bass tackle is an 11 ft (3.35 m) rod weighing 16 oz (450 g) or less in glass or carbon fibre and a light reel – a multiplier is best. If the reef is free of line-cutting barnacles and flints, fish 10–15 lb (4.50–6.50 kg) line.

Casting distance isn't important on most reefs. Bass are happy to forage wherever there is about 2 ft (60 cm) of water over their back. If such a depth exists just 10 ft (3 m) out from your rock ledge, and the fauna suggests bass will hunt through there, try lobbing a crab out and keeping out of sight. You may be surprised. Bass will hunt right at the edge of a flooding tide. Do much rock

Watch out for the flooding tide!

Surf fishing for bass along the Sussex coast.

bassing and the chances are that one day you'll see a bass cruising along the edge of a reef with its dorsal fin out of the water.

After casting out, very gingerly tighten the line until there's reasonable tension on it and you can feel the sinker. If you tighten too much, or drag the sinker to make sure it is not snagged, you'll pull it into a crevice and maybe tangle the hook around a weed stem, thereby ensuring complete failure. If no bites come, wind down the rod tip until it is pointing along the line, yet without shifting the sinker. Now strike smartly upwards, pulling the tackle off the sea-bed and wind like hell. A high-speed reel is vital here to bring the gear to the surface and out of reach of the graunch.

Rock bass bites vary from tiny twitches to full-blooded pulls. Sometimes big bass play with a crab running off with it, dropping it, running again, then just as you strike, they drop it again. You need to be very lucky to make contact with these. Equally weird is the bass that picks up the crab and shakes it, drops it again, picks it up once more and shakes it like a dog worrying an old glove.

As a general rule, most bass that signal on the rod top in a determined manner have the bait well down inside their mouth and should be struck immediately. That is why a rod-rest is out of place on a bass reef. The rod should be held all the time. Bass have large mouths, but a crab bait larger than a standard match-box is less easy for them to inhale. A suspicious fish may be spooked while trying to cram an outsize bait into its mouth. Provided a reasonable bait is oozing juices, it is big enough. Beyond this point the law of diminishing returns takes effect. Big baits may just be carried off between bass lips, away from competing fish, in the same way as a sea-gull flies off with a whole mackerel in order to choke it back at the edge of the flock.

Chapter 13
Bottom-feeders, wrasse and mullet

Flounders

Flounders can be caught all the year round but the winter months bring the largest catches especially from the English Channel coast. After a gale, the flounders invade the storm beaches in this area in search of the many shellfish which have been gouged from their shells. At this time baits such as razorfish, cockles and butterfish can be used with great effectiveness. At other times, the best general baits are peeler crab and white or red ragworm. Flounders are very inquisitive and are attracted by movement. For this reason, ragworms are effective when fished in clear water. They should be mounted on the hook so that the tails wriggle.

The flounder spoon is a highly favoured method among dinghy anglers who fish in estuaries and along sheltered beaches. It is less effective from the shore and its success is very localized. In general, a flounder spoon is of white plastic or chromed brass/steel about the size of a tablespoon – locally larger on occasions. This is mounted at the end of a short trace via a swivel with the hook

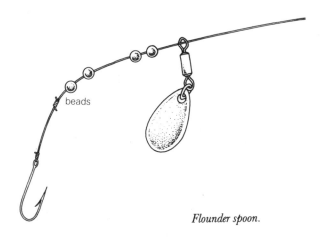

Flounder spoon.

tied 4–6 in (10–15 cm) behind the spoon. This is baited with ragworm, and so on. As the tackle is retrieved slowly across the bottom, the spoon flutters and kicks up the sand, which arouses the fish's interest. I suspect that when the spoon does work its vibrations are also an attraction. That is the theory, but in reality few shore anglers will give the baited spoon any thought because it is rarely as deadly as normal legering techniques.

The most effective method of flounder fishing is with a large piece of peeler crab that is oozing juices, mounted on a size 1/0 Mustad 79510 or size 2 Spearspade. This is cast out and retrieved by inches at intervals, and I mean inches! When worm baits are used, a size 6–2 Aberdeen or Kirby longshank is ideal. It is surprising how big a bait a flounder can engulf in its mouth. A 1 lb (0.45 kg) fish can take a golf-ball-size bait, but it can't spit the hook out so easily, so once the hook is inside, he is invariably caught.

Flounder bites vary between short plucks and rod-bending runs. They should never be struck and as is the case with all flatfish, time is the key to success. Left to their own devices, flounders will hook themselves.

With strong teeth, a large mouth, and efficient camouflage, the turbot is an effective predator.

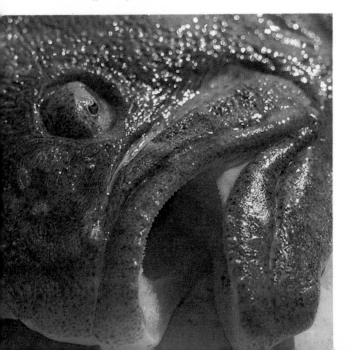

119

Plaice

This species is best sought by legering on the sea-bed – either a flowing trace or a mono paternoster can be employed. Hook size depends on bait being used. Longshank size 1 or 2 hooks are best for worm baits and shortshank 2/0 for peeler crab. This bait is especially useful for the bigger fish, and other baits worth using include lugworm, king ragworm, harbour ragworm, mussel and other molluscs. Plaice are often found in large numbers over mussel beds – where they are quickly caught by trawlers.

Plaice are the one flatfish which rarely feed at night. Some of the best catches come at dusk, but as soon as darkness falls they stop feeding. They can be caught all through the summer, but during the early months of the season they are in very poor condition, having just spawned. Unfortunately this is the time when they are easiest to catch as they feed ravenously. During July and August, however, plaice are fat and in prime condition. As they are reeled in, they hug the bottom and then appear in the surf at the last minute, deflecting the water to force themselves down.

Turbot

The turbot grows to about 30 lb (14 kg), with a 15 lb (6.8 kg) fish being an excellent shore-caught specimen. Turbot are predominantly fish-eaters and can be caught on mackerel strip, sand-eels and herring. Large fish occasionaly take small fish that have hooked themselves (i.e., pouting and whiting) without the angler being aware. Leger tackle should be used with a simple, one-hook, running paternoster most successful. For fish baits, hooks up to size 3/0 are ideal. The turbot, in common with all fish-eaters, has a large mouth and a 5 lb (2.2 kg) fish can easily engulf half a fillet of mackerel.

The summer months produce most turbot with September and November giving the southern-based angler the chance of a rare large specimen.

Dabs

Dabs feed on the many minute creatures found on the sea-bed and are rarely caught with lugworm in their stomachs. Anglers, however, find that lugworm is by far the most successful bait for dabs. Many swear by stale black lugworm as the killer bait. The best tackle is either a flowing trace or a paternoster. When this species is dense inshore, some anglers use a three-hook paternoster and take them three at a time, arguing that best sport is had from dabs not with a fishing rod but with a knife and fork in their hands. Hooks should be small – size 2 is ideal for use with lugworm. An excellent summer bait is the peeled legs of a peeler crab. This is particularly successful when crabs are removing lugworm quickly as it will stay on the hook longer because crabs, although cannibalistic, do not eat their own kind all of the time. During the spring and autumn when dabs are following the sprat shoals, a cocktail of lugworm and strip of sprat can prove deadly.

Sole

The sole feeds ravenously in the dark and often swims very close to the shoreline. Shoals are often of fish of an average size with the bigger specimens loners. If you catch one, there is a good chance of others. The most successful bait is black lugworm. Leger tackle should be used and the best rig is a flowing trace. Hooks should be small – size 4–6 is ideal for worm baits. Sole fishing is a waiting game, and sport can be either non-existent or hectic. Often they are present in large numbers but aren't feeding. When one feeds they all feed. Their favourite time for feeding is the two hours before dawn or during those times when the direction of the tide is changing. Soles bury themselves in the sand when the tide is flowing strongly, but swim out to turn around and face the other way when the new current starts to flow. It is at this time that they will often feed for a brief period.

The breams

Only two members of this family are commonly caught in British waters, and these mainly in the English Channel and around some southern areas of Ireland.

Of the two species regularly caught in British waters, the red bream is the most common but it is a deep-water fish. The shore angler is likely to encounter only small specimens, weighing up to 1 lb (450 g). Its cousin, the black bream is rarely caught in large numbers from the shore except in a few areas of the south and west of Britain and from the Channel Isles. In other areas, the occasional specimen turns up during the summer months and this will often be a respectable fish of 2–3 lb (900 g–1.3 kg). Both types of bream grow to around 6lb (2.7kg), and a 3lb (1.3kg) specimen is a good one. Preferred habitat is rocky ground, although shoals will roam widely over many types of sea-bed except open sand.

Favourite baits for bream are king rag, lugworm, slim strips of squid, sand-eels, mackerel strip and peeler crab. They are caught over rough ground and from piers, usually down the side of the wall or piles. Bream feed on the bottom and in mid-water so both leger and float tackle can be used. Fishing from rocks with a sliding float will reveal the excellent qualities of this species. Their shape affords them both power and manoeuvrability and they put up a good scrap. Bream have small mouths so bait and hooks should be small.

Gurnard

The family of gurnards contains four fish which can be caught in British waters. They feed mainly on the bottom and are mostly found over soft sea-beds. However, a swarm of fry will induce them to rise up and give chase, sometimes even breaking the surface like mackerel. But this is rare.

Gurnards are rarely sought on purpose by the shore angler. Because they are bottom-feeders and inhabit open ground they are very susceptible to the trawl and are comparatively rare. They are highly prized as eating fish. The grey is found mainly in the south but does venture all round the British coastline, whereas the tub is rarely caught

Soles are bearded with tiny barbels called 'villi', with which they locate prey.

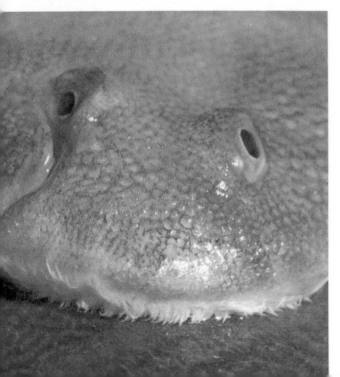

in northern seas. The red gurnard is a fish of the south and west. These species are usually caught on baits and leger tackle intended for flatfish or whiting.

The weevers

This family contains two species that are the only poisonous British fish. The lesser weever is the commonest – and the smallest – and the one most likely to be caught by the shore angler. Its poison can cause considerable pain. It averages 4in (10cm) in length. It is silvery with a dark brown back, a stumpy head and long anal fin which reaches its tail. The front dorsal fin, which consists of a row of venomous hypodermic needles, is black and often has a yellow spot on it.

The greater weever is a deep-water species and is rarely caught from the shore. It grows to about 2lb (900g) and is as deadly as its smaller brother.

Wrasse

Seven species of wrasse are found round British shores. Cuckoo wrasse grow to around 2lb (900g), but are found in deeper water where boat anglers classify them as a nuisance. So ballan wrasse are the ones that command the attention of the British angler. Not only do they grow quite large (they've been caught commercially to 20lb (9kg), if such reports are accurate), but they are also readily available close inshore.

Wrasse are the inhabitants of deep water and undercut ledges out of the light. In this sheltered world they feed no matter how hot and bright the weather. Tackle doesn't need to be chosen for casting but to match the fish's fighting ability and the ruggedness of its environment. A powerful carp rod or light bass rod can be used where the fish grow to around 4lb (1.8kg). Where fish of 5lb (2.2kg) and over are to be found a stronger rod, which will cast up to 4oz (115g), is needed. Line of 10lb (4.50kg) is ideal for the first outfit, 18lb (8kg) for the second. It should be a hard grade of nylon to withstand the abrasive environment. The only reel worth using is a multiplier, as a fixed-spool reel makes a poor winch.

Terminal rigs need to be easily made and cheap to replace. Wrasse jungle claims plenty of tackle because the only place to fish is right in the thick of it. If you cast out into clearer water you'll catch few fish, and they'll be juveniles. A leader is a waste of time, for the obvious reasons. Tie hooks to a length of 20lb (9kg) line to take abrasion from teeth. Other tackle should be tied direct to the main line.

There is one rig that suffices for wrasse, with two variations – a paternoster, or one supported by a float. Tie 4ft (1.2m) of weak line to a swivel fixed to the end of the main line. Tie on an old sparking plug – or whatever – as a weight. Tie 2ft (60cm) or less of 20lb (9kg) line to the top eye of the swivel and end this with a strong, forged hook around 1/0 size. Only one at a time here – two or more hooks is courting disaster.

Some days the wrasse will be a long way down the rock face, at other times they'll be higher in the water. It pays to fish at different depths until the fish are found, though groundbait can influence matters considerably. The main food of wrasse is crustaceans, molluscs and fry.

Wrasse can be caught on spinners, flies and red-gills, but the frustration of continuously breaking free from snags, and the cost, make this a better way of losing red-gills than of catching

With rabbit-like front teeth for eating barnacles and mussels, and a coat of tough scales, wrasse are well equipped to live in rock tangles.

wrasse. A better system is to floatfish small strips of mackerel, sand-eels, squid or small rock fish, though a bait with smell appeal works best.

Groundbait is a great help at times. Whether you throw in spoonfuls of tinned cat food, handfuls of crunched crabs or loose-feed with stale lug, the effect can be spectacular. In hotspots, groundbait is not necessary as the fish are so populous. The smell of the bait alone is enough to bring them around.

Bites normally consist of a couple of tugs and a solid pull. If the fish keeps plucking, slowly draw the bait away to provoke a positive take. Ideally, the clutch of the reel should have been adjusted prior to fishing so that it slips at a firm, but safe pressure. The first dive of a hooked wrasse is impressively powerful. Hold on tight, and yield line only if it is likely to pop if you don't – you must prevent the fish getting back to its hole. With very big ones, however, line has to be given. If a fish regains cover, slacken off completely for a couple of minutes and try to con the fish into believing it has escaped, and into coming back out again. However, that is not much good if the fish has already wound the line twice round a thick kelp stem. The more vertically you can fish over a wrasse hole, the better will be your success rate.

By pointing the rod down the line, you can strike and lift in one movement, thereby taking it by surprise before it starts fighting. Once the first dive has been controlled, the fish is virtually beaten.

When rock fishing, a landing net is not really practical, neither is a drop-net. Both get swirled about by the surf. The best way to land a wrasse is to wind down to the fish, then smoothly swing it ashore. If it drops off, well, it would have been put back anyway.

Mullet

To the practised eye, the three British species are easy to tell apart. Most of the mullet caught around the British Isles are of the thick-lipped variety ('thick'), so-named after its gristly rubber-tyre of an upper lip. It differs from the thin-lipped ('thin') in that the jugular interspace (the area where the gill covers meet under the chin) is narrow and parallel. That of the thin is wide and oval, and its upper lip is less large. Other differences become noticeable with experience. The golden-grey ('goldie') looks similar to the thin, but prefers open sea, while thins are normally caught well upstream in estuaries. It has a large golden spot on the gill cover and a thick coat of mucous over its body, neither of which are found on the thin. May to October sees the peak of the mullet season in most areas, with June-August being the most profitable months.

In the case of thicks and thins, the angler's task is to wean the fish off their diet of plankton, small molluscs, crustaceans and worms, so that they will accept a food item that can be mounted on to the hook. This involves ground baiting, and also allows him to choose a bait that is convenient to use. Finely-minced fish, mashed bread (remove air bubbles or it will float) and, for thins, surface mud, all produce the required effect. A thin cloud in the water is not enough, though. They have to be educated into accepting particles of the right size. So bait-sized pieces of bread, fish and so on, have to be included. The intention is to re-programme the fish, not to feed them. One idea for thicks is to pulverize several canfuls of sweetcorn in a liquidizer, then add a tin of whole grains, the mixture being introduced to the fishing area on the little-and-often basis that is so vital to success.

Mullet tackle owes more to coarse fishing than to sea angling. An 11–13 ft (3.35–3.95 m) match rod, a small fixed-spool reel, 3–6 lb (1.35–2.70 kg)

Rough and ragged wrasse country. Keith Roberts primes his hook.

line, sizes 8–12 hooks, freshwater-type floats, landing net and ancilliary gear are suitable for fishing from piers and in harbours, marinas and estuaries. Much of the time, freshwater float-fishing and paternostering tactics produce best results.

Thins bite very fast as a rule and it is vital to hit them as the float flashes under water. Thicks give all manner of bites. Sometimes the float lies flat. At other times it slowly slides away. Experience is required before correct interpretation of these movements is possible. A float that is locked on to the line with a split shot each side of the wire loop at the base of the stem makes less surface disturbance on the strike than one clamped to the line with rubber rings.

Thin-lips like to live high up estuaries, where fresh water meets salt.

Stick to floats and shotting patterns that produce results. Thorough familiarity with the behaviour of your end tackle enables you to recognize and interpret its characteristic movements.

It is essential that you learn to interpret mullet behaviour. All too often, anglers find shoals of them cavorting about the river, harbour or wherever, and become more and more frustrated as these blatantly visible fish refuse so much as to nibble at the bait. This is often because the fish aren't interested in food. Feeding mullet are often out of sight – their natural food lies on the sea-bed.

Those meandering about aimlessly near the surface are rarely interested in food. While those below, out of sight, are busy tucking into the carpet of groundbait. In harbours where thicks rest under boats and pontoons, it is sometimes possible to tempt a few to venture out. Obviously when thicks are seduced by floating bread they can be seen to feed.

Mullet have tough mouths and strikes must be positive. If the line has sunk, strike sideways rather than upwards so as not to frighten fish by ripping it through the surface.

Thick-lipped mullet.

Thin-lipped mullet.

Index

Page numbers in italic refer to illustrations

accessories 56
acid water 68
alkaline water 68
antenna 33
Appetiser 64
Arlesey bomb *37, 39*
Avon (Hampshire) 19, 22

baits:
  coarse 6-16, 39
  dead 22, 26, *49, 50*
  live 26, *49, 50*
  shore 95-101
bait clip 90
balsas 30, 32, *32*
barbel *18,* 19
bass *86-7,* 114-8, *116*
  baits 94, 115, 118
  fishing methods 115-6, 117-8
  surf fishing 114
  tackle 115, *116*
Beacon Beige 65
Black and Peacock Spider 59
Black Gnat 69
Black Lure 59
Black Marabou 59, *60,* 64
Black Midge pupa 59
Black Pennell 62
Blue and Silver 71
boat fishing 61, 73
  tackle 56
Bob Church's Appetiser 59
bomb 90
bread 12, 19, 21, 22, 39
bream 121
bream, bronze *14,* 19-20, *21*
  location 20
  tackle 20
brown trout *see* trout
bullets 90
Bumbles 79
Butcher 62, 71

caddis *60,* 64
carp 13, 20-2, *23*
  baits 21-2
  tackle 22

casters 10, 41
casting 56-7, 61, 92-4, *93*
  pendulum 92
  South African 92
  Yarmouth 92
chalk-streams 66, 68, 69, 70
cheese 22
chub 19, 22, *24-5*
  tackle 22
Cinnamon Sedge 64
Coch-y-Bondhu 65
cod 92-4, 112-4, *112, 113*
  baits 114
  fishing methods 114
  pier fishing 114
  rock fishing 114
  tackle 112
conger eel 106-8, *106*
  baits 107
  fishing methods 107-8
  landing 107-8
  tackle 107
crab 98-9, *98*
craneflies (daddy-long-legs) 64
crayfish 22
crook 44, *45*

dabs 120
dace 22
daddy-long-legs *see* craneflies
damselfly nymph *60,* 64
Derwent 39
dogfish 104
double-taper line 54
drogue 56, 71
droppers 62
ducker 33, 35
Dunkeld 62

eel 22
  baits 22
  tackle 22

feeding 12-16
fish baits 99-100, 123
fish location 66
fixed paternoster 91, *91*

flick tip 44
float rig 91, *91*
floatfishing 8, 26, *28-9,* 30-5
floating line 54-5
flotant 62
flounder 94, 119
  spoon *119*
Foster, Freddie 35

garfish *109,* 110
Gold-ribbed Hare's Ear 69
gozzer 10
Grafham Water 53
grayling 79-81, *80*
  fishing methods 79-81
  tackle 79
Great Ouse Relief Channel 27
Great Red Sedge 64
Green Insect 79
Greenwell's Glory 69
Grey Duster 65
groundbait 15-6, 20, 39, 40, 41, 123
Grousewing 64
gudgeon 26
gurnard 121

Hart, Johnny 35
hemp 10, 19, 22
herring fry 73
hooks 8-9, 39, 89
  sinking the 68-9

Iron Blue 65, 68, 69

Lake Olive 61
landing net 56, 65
Large Dark Olive 80
leads 90, *90*
lead-clip 90
leaders 55-6, 59, 61, 71-2, 74-5, 79
leger rig 91, *91*
legering 8, 26, 35-41
  in running water 39-40
  methods 39
  tackle 35-9
  terminal rigs 39
light 90

line
    coarse 7, 26, 30, 40, 35-9
    fly 53, *54*, 55, 59, 61, 64, 71, 73, 74-5, 79
    shore 88-9, 103, 107, 112-3, 114, 116, 122, 125
lobworm 10
loose feed 12-5
lugworm 95, *96-7*
Lunn's Caperer 69
lure fishing 59-61, 62
lures *60*, 64, 100-1

mackerel 108-10
    bait 108-10
    behaviour 108
    fishing methods 110
    tackle 110
maggots 9, 16, 19, 21, 22, 26, 39, 40, 41
Marks, Ivan 35
Medium Olive 69
midge larva 64
midge pupa *60*, 61, 64
missiles 33
Muddler Minnow 64
mullet 123-5
    baits 125
    fishing methods 125
    golden 123
    tackle 125
    thick-lipped 123, *125*
    thin-lipped 123, *125*

nymph *60*
nymph fshing *58*, *63*, 68-9

Orange Midge pupa 59

Pale Watery Olive 69, 80
paternoster rig *31*
perch 26
Peter Ross 71
Pheasant Tail Nymph 59, *60*, 61, 64, 65, 69, 81
pike 26, 27, 47-50, *48*
    baits *49*, 50
    tackle 47-50
pinkies 10, 26, 40
plaice 120
pole fishing 41-6, *45*
    terminal rigs 46
poles 7, 41-6
    take-apart 44
    telescopic 46
pollack 110-2, *111*
    baits 110
    fishing methods 110-2
    tackle 110
Pond Olive *60*, 61
prawns 100
Price's Orange Streamer 61

quivertip 20, 35-9, *38*, 40

ragworm 95-8
rainbow trout *see* trout
rain-fed rivers 68
rays 104-6, *105*
    baits 104
    fishing methods 104-6
    location 104
    tackle 104
Red Sedge 64
Red Tag 79
red worm 10
reels 7-8, *8*, 55, 75, 83-8, 115, 125
rivers 39-40, 55, 66-70
    see also seatrout, trout
roach 26
rod rest 35-7, 89
rods:
    coarse 7, 22, 26, 35
    fly 51-3, *51*, 55, 59, 61, 65, 67, 70, 71, 73, 74, 79
    shore 82-3, 103, 104, 107, 112-3, 114, 116, 122, 125
Rogan's Golden Olive 62
rudd 26
running paternoster 90, *91*, 103
Rutland Water 53

salmon 74-8, *75*, *77*
    fishing methods 76-8
    tackle 74-6
sand-eel 73, 101, 123
Sargasso Sea 22
Sawyer's Killer Bug 81
seatrout 71-4, *72*
    fishing methods 71-4
    in estuaries 73-4
    in rivers 71-3
    in stillwaters 73
    tackle 71-4
sedge *see* caddis
Sepia Dun 61
Severn 15, 19, 39, 40
shallow-water beaches 114
shellfish baits 99
shooting-taper line 54
shot 90
shotting *21*, 32, 33-5
shrimps 64, 73, 100
Silver Midge pupa 59
Silver Sedge 64
sinking line 54-5, 61
sink-tip line 54-5
sliding link *37*, *41*
slugs 22
snails 22, 64
sole 121, *121*
spate streams 70
Spey 71
spinning paternoster 91
sprats 73

springtip 20, 35-9
squatts 10, 26
steep shingle beaches 113
stick float 26, 30-5, *30*, *31*, *32*
stickfly 59
stillwaters 51-5, 58-65
    see also seatrout, trout
sting-rays 106
Stour (Dorset) 19
Sweeney Todd 59
sweetcorn 12, 21
swimfeeder 19, 20, 40-1, *40*, *41*
    blockend 40
    methods of fishing 41
    open-ended 40
    tackle 40
swingtip 20, 35-9, *36*
swivels 89-90

tackle 7-9, 35-9, 40, 51-7, 70, 82-9, *89*
    see also individual species
tares 10
target board 35
Teal 71
tench 26-7, *27*, 50
terminal rigs 39, 46, 90-1, 122
tope *102*, 103
Treacle Parkin 79
Trent 15, 19, 21, 22, 39
trout 51-70, *67*
    behaviour 58
    choice of fly 68-9
    choice of tackle 59-61
    feeding patterns 66
    in rivers 66-70
    in stillwaters 58-65
    location 66
    methods of fishing 59-70
    tackle 51-7
Tup's Indispensable 65
turbot 120, *120*

waggler 26, 30-5, *33*, *34*
    choice of 35
Walton, Izaak 35
wasp grub 12, 22
weavers 122
weight-forward line 54
Welland 22
Welshman's Button 64
wheat 12
Whisky 59
White Marabou 59, *60*, 64
worms 8, 10, 19, 21, 22, 39
wrasse 91. 122, *122*, *123*
Wye 22

yellow-tail lugworm 95

zander 26, 27
zoomer 35